NICHOLAS ROMANOV

Life and Death

Liki Rossii
St Petersburg
1998

NICHOLAS ROMANOV
Life and Death

By Yuri Shelayev, Elizabeth Shelayeva
and Nicholas Semenov

Selection of photographs: Liudmila Protsai

Designer: Vladimir Bukhanov

Translated from the Russian by Paul Williams

Computer typesetting:
A.V. Illarionov, A. Ye. Platonov
Editor: M. V. Irkhina

This publication makes use of photographs from
the Central State Archive of Cinematic, Photographic and Phonographic Documents in St Petersburg
and the National Library of Russia.

ISBN 5-87417-065-0

Printed and bound in Germany, Leipzig,
Neumann & Nuernberger
Films by AMOS, St Petersburg

When, on 14 May 1896, the young Russian ruler Nicholas II was solemnly crowned Tsar of All the Russias, there can hardly have been a single person among the many thousands who crowded around the ancient Assumption Cathedral in the Moscow Kremlin who thought for a moment that they were witnessing the end of a centuries-old tradition. Before a host of eager eyes the last of Russia's autocrats was formally invested with his awesome power in a ceremony that went back to 1547 and Ivan the Terrible. There were still four days left to the Khodynka Field catastrophe that was to cast its gloomy shadow over all the subsequent years of Nicholas's reign, and everything seemed to favour the new monarch as perhaps never before.

His reign, met with hopes and expectations, began in a period of astonishing calm in both domestic affairs and international relations throughout Europe. Russia was experiencing an unprecedented economic upswing and the political turmoil that followed the great reforms under Alexander II seemed a thing of the distant past. Nevertheless, with every successive year the country, at first imperceptibly, but still ineluctably, was headed for a tremendous catastrophe.

The causes of such a fateful turn in Russia's destiny and the degree of Nicholas II's personal responsibility for the tragic outcome of his reign are hard to determine even today, although a truly immense body of literature — both memoirs and researches — has been devoted to those questions. The aim of this book is not to conduct yet another re-examination of history; it merely invites you to look again through the pages of the tragic life of the last Russian Emperor and to examine the faces of those who were close to him.

The Imperial Winter Palace.
St Petersburg. 1900s.
Photograph by K. Bulla

Childhood and Growing up

Grand Duke Nicholas Alexandrovich was the first child of Tsesarevich Alexander Alexandrovich (the future Alexander III) and his wife Maria Fiodorovna, the former Danish Princess Dagmar. He came into the world on 6 May 1868, on the day when the Orthodox Church commemorates the Old Testament figure of Job "the Long-Suffering". This became a portent for that strange sense of doom that many around him noted. During the difficult years of his reign, the Emperor referred to the coincidence on several occasions, speaking of his inner preparedness to suffer the trials that befell him one after another in his public and private life.

That was all in the future, however. For the moment fate seemed to have granted Nicholas an exceptionally happy childhood and youth. His upbringing differed from that of the majority of his crowned predecessors in being much more family-oriented, more "homely". Tsesarevich (a title given to the Russian heir apparent) Alexander Alexandrovich and his wife evidently preferred the intimated, cosy world of their own family to the glamorous, but in many ways cold and stiffly formal life of St Petersburg high society. Perhaps for that reason, for the young Nicholas, and for his younger brothers and sisters, his parents were above all "papa" and "mama", and not imperious figures at the pinnacle of an immense state, as, for example, his formidable grandfather Nicholas I was for his children.

The atmosphere of simplicity, sincerity and warmth that reigned in the Anichkov Palace was to a large extent responsible for the highly appealing human aspects of the last autocrat's character. His exceptional personal charm was unanimously noted later, even by those who were highly critical of his behaviour as a statesman.

Yet the Grand Duke's untroubled early years also had their dangerous side: for someone destined to become the ruler of one of the world's great empires, Nicholas too long, almost to the moment when he ascended the throne, retained a perception of life that might be said to be limited by his nursery walls. Many contemporaries also noted a certain infantile aspect to his mental make up.

Grand Duke Nicholas Alexandrovich. 1872

His interests in life were limited to a small circle of intimates. In their company he found the necessary support and even protection from a unknown and frightening world, whose hostility was already making itself clearly felt to the Russian imperial family even as Nicholas grew up.

With every successive decade the mood in the nation's public life became ever more threatening for the inhabitants of the imperial palaces. Shortly before Nicholas was born, an unprecedented event took place. When Dmitry Karakozov fired at Alexander II in April 1866 it literally stunned the Russian people — a mere mortal had raised his hand against God's Anointed. A year later a Polish émigré named Berezowski shot at the Emperor during his visit to Paris.

The aura of near-mystic veneration that had surrounded royal power in Russia since ancient times was melting rapidly away. Only recently the Russian autocrats had been able to stroll practically unguarded along the banks of the Neva and the streets around the Winter Palace, responding to the greetings of the passers-by. By the late 1870s that was simply impossible — the Tsar was literally a hunted man. In April 1879 Alexander Solovyev loosed off five bullets at the Emperor from close range, but failed to hit him. Towards the end of that year, on 18 November, the "People's Will" group tried to blow up the imperial train, wrecking a stretch of railway. The Tsar had, however, already passed the spot. At six in the evening of 5 February 1880, the very time when the royal family were due to enter the dining-room, an explosion rocked the Winter Palace itself. The man behind it was Stepan Khalturin who had gained access to the palace as a stoker and managed little by little to smuggle enough dynamite into the room below. Again it was only a stroke of fortune that the Emperor was not hurt.

Nonetheless, on 1 March 1881, the death sentenced passed by the executive committee of People's Will was carried out. The mysterious prediction of the fortune-teller who once told Alexander II that there would be seven attempts on his life had come true.

This tragedy was an important turning-point in the formation of Nicholas's character and personality. Together with his younger brother Georgy he was present at his grandfather's deathbed. "My father took me up to the bed," the last Emperor would recall. "Papa," he said, raising his voice, 'your ray of sunshine is here.' I saw the eyelashes tremble. My grandfather's eyes opened. He was trying to smile. He moved a finger. He could not raise his hands, nor say what he wanted to, but he undoubtedly recognised me..."

The shock of this experience would remain with Nicholas to the end of his days. Even in distant Tobolsk he remembered it. "The anniversary of Apap's [Alexander II's] death," he wrote in his diary on 1 March 1918. "At two o'clock a memorial service was held for us here. The weather was the same as it was then — frosty and sunny."

Alexander II with Empress Maria Alexandrovna. 1860s

Alexander II (1818–1881), Nicholas II's grandfather, has gone down in history as the Tsar-Liberator. He was one of the most outstanding statesmen in nineteenth-century Russia and his reign has come to be known as "the period of great reforms". The eldest son of Emperor Nicholas I, he was given an wide-ranging European-style education and was profoundly aware of the necessity of making serious changes to the prevailing state of affairs in Russia. The greatest event of his reign was the signing of the Manifesto of 19 February 1861 which liberated the serfs. This question had been a burden on the country for over a century and all his predecessors had shrunk from it in irresolution before he final took a decisive step. By a bitter irony of fate, however, Alexander II was killed a few hours after he signed a draft law that envisaged the beginnings of representation in the central administration of the Russian state. For all the limited nature of the proposed reforms, it could have become the first step towards the empire becoming a constitutional monarchy. The bomb thrown by the terrorist Ignaty Grinevitsky on the Catherine Canal embankment fatally wounded the Emperor and wiped out any hope that a peaceful change of political course was possible. The murder of the Tsar became a powerful argument for the conservatives who sought to prevent any reforms in Russia.

NICHOLAS ROMANOV. Life and Death

The death of the Tsar-Liberator overturned the traditional pattern of life at the imperial court. Alexander III disliked the Winter Palace and it stood empty, used only as the venue for official ceremonies and grand court balls. As a rule, the new Emperor preferred the more modest Anichkov Palace on Nevsky Prospekt to which he was accustomed, having lived there while still Tsesarevich. Gradually, however, the new chief residence of his reign became the isolated fortress-palace situated in the relatively remote town of Gatchina, some thirty miles outside St Petersburg. It seemed the most reliable retreat in the present troubled times. Increased security, special safety measures whenever the family moved from place to place, and contact only with the extremely small circle of people that his autocrat father allowed to get close — all this left a lasting mark on Nicholas. In 1884, on the eve of his coming-of-age, the secretary of state Polovtsov confided to his diary that "in view of the unvaried, secluded life of the sovereign's sons, the heir to the throne should have been given the opportunity to see more people." The Emperor's response to such suggestions was that "his sons see those people who visit him, but regrettably he is visited by members of a single, narrow clique."

That is not to say that Nicholas did not have his own circle of acquaintances. He certainly did, and apart from his brothers and his first cousins once removed Grand Dukes Alexander and Sergei Mikhailovich, there were young people of his own age — the children of two of his father's intimates, Count Sheremetev and Count Vorontsov-Dashkov, the minister of the court. The members of this youthful company got the nickname "potatoes" from the potatoes baked in the embers of a bonfire that were a favourite ending to summer evenings in the Gatchina park. This little group retained its childish character for too long, however. Even as an adult, just two years from the throne, Nicholas could spend a whole evening with one of the "potatoes" playing hide-and-seek or chase.

Alexander III. St Petersburg. Early 1880s

Alexander III (1845–1894) was fated to become Russian Emperor as the result of two major tragedies for the House of Romanov. The untimely death of his elder brother, Tsesarevich Nicholas Alexandrovich, from galloping consumption in April 1865, made him heir to the throne; the untimely death of his father, Alexander II, at the hands of the People's Will on 1 March 1881, that terrible day for the whole of Russia, ushered in his reign.

Fulfilling the last will of his brother, in October 1866 Alexander married the late Tsesarevich's fiancée, Dagmar of Denmark, and the marriage proved a very happy one, something rare among crowned heads. On the other hand, Alexander rejected the political testament of his murdered father, who on his last morning had signed a manifesto signifying the start of gradual constitutional changes in autocratic Russia, and his reign was marked by a reaction against the great reforms of the previous twenty years.

This kind and considerate paterfamilias, who was at the same time overbearing and intolerant of contradiction, displayed those same traits of character in his patriarchal attitude to the government of the country. The despotic aspect of his rule was hard to swallow even for many who shared his political ideas. Contemporary accounts suggest that more than any other Romanov Alexander III embodied the traditional popular conception of a real Russian Tsar. A powerfully built giant with a brown beard who towered above any crowd, he seemed the embodiment of the might and dignity of Russia. His popularity was to a large extent founded on his fidelity to the nation's traditions and interests.

Nobody expected that his life would prove so short, curtailed by kidney disease. A fateful role may have been played by the crash of the royal train on 17 October 1888 when Alexander III received serious contusions in the area of the lower back.

Grand Duke Tsesarevich Alexander Alexandrovich. London. 1870s.
Photograph by «Maul & Co»

**Empress Maria Fiodorovna, wife of Alexander III.
St Petersburg. 1881. Photograph by A. Pasetti**

Empress Maria (1847–1928) — Marie Sophie Frederike Dagmar until she adopted Orthodoxy — was the fourth child of King Christian IX, founder of the Glücksberg dynasty in Denmark, and his consort Queen Louise. Her marriage to Grand Duke Alexander Alexandrovich produced six children: Nicholas, Alexander (who died in infancy), Georgy, Xenia, Mikhail and Olga. In her youth Maria Fiodorovna was an exceptional beauty, lively and sociable with a light-hearted nature.

The premature demise of her husband in October 1894 placed her in a difficult position. While in the early years of her son's reign the Dowager Empress continued to be in Nicholas's eyes a guardian of his father's precepts and the autocrat rarely undertook anything without consulting her, subsequently her influence waned appreciably. This was in no small part due to her relationship with her daughter-in-law, which was strained from the start and always remained exceptionally cool and formal.

As time went on the alienation between the two imperial courts became ever more evident. Maria Fiodorovna was an implacable opponent of Rasputin's influence, considering his appearance among the imperial family a death blow to the dynasty.

She observed with sorrow the headlong decline in the standing of the monarchy, the prestige of which the late Alexander III had exerted such efforts to enhance. The father's legacy proved beyond the son's powers and an awareness of this fact, so tragic for the Russian monarchy, became a grave burden in Maria Fiodorovna's later years.

On 21 March 1917 the Dowager Empress left for the Crimea where she lived for two years with her daughters Olga and Xenia and several grand duke, who gathered in one of the Romanovs' summer residences. In April 1919 they left Russia for ever on board a British cruiser, sent for them at the request of Queen Alexandra, widow of King Edward VII and Maria Fiodorovna's sister.

The former Russian Empress spent her last years in Copenhagen, short of funds and with only a few people around her.

Nicholas was a physically strong, very lively and full of stamina. He walked a great deal without tiring. He could get up to mischief at times, but on the whole displayed a calm, gentle character. Rather reserved and restrained in the expression of his feelings, he found it hard to let others get close to him. Much later Count Sheremetev observed that, although his own children had in their early years been "playmates ... of the heir to the throne, none of them was capable of saying what his way of thinking was." To some extent this character trait is reflected in the dispassionate, even rather dry entries we find in the diary which he began in his teens, in 1882, and conscientiously kept to the end of his days. For the most part the events of the day are recorded laconically without comment. His personal emotions, thoughts and feelings remained as a rule hidden deep inside him and only his letters to those closest to him — his mother, Alexandra Fiodorovna, and Grand Duke Alexander Mikhailovich — display him to have been an emotionally alive, even passionate man.

Grand Duke Nicholas Alexandrovich. 1870s

The family of Alexander III: (standing left to right) Maria Fiodorovna embracing Grand Duke Mikhail, Grand Duke Nicholas and Grand Duchess Xenia, (seated) Alexander III holding Grand Duchess Olga and Grand Duke Georgy. St Petersburg. 1888–90. Photograph by Levitsky

NICHOLAS ROMANOV. Life and Death

Since Nicholas was destined from birth to hold the supreme position in the state, his education and upbringing were the objects of the most fixed attention. Systematic instruction began for him at the age of eight following a special programme devised by Adjutant General Danilovich, whom Alexander III entrusted with supervision of Nicholas's studies. The programme was divided into two parts. The course of general education, planned for eight years, corresponded in general terms to that of the *gymnasia* (grammar schools), although with substantial modifications. It is a curious fact that while both Alexander II and the future Alexander III wholeheartedly supported the movement to reform the gymnasium education with more teaching of the classical languages, Greek and Latin, as well as mathematics, those subjects were not included in the programme to prepare the future Tsar. Instead he received extended instruction in political history, rissian literature, geography and the basis of mineralogy and biology. Particular emphasis in the first eight years was placed on studying modern European languages. Nicholas had a perfect mastery of English and French; lesser fluency in German and Danish. From childhood he loved historical literature and fiction, which he read in both Russian and foreign languages, and even admitted that "if I was a private individual, I would devote myself to historical researches." With time his particular tastes in literature established themselves: Nicholas was fond of browsing in Pushkin, Gogol and Lermontov, while he loved Leo Tolstoy, Dostoyevsky and Chekhov.

The course of higher education, originally intended for four years, and then extended to five, included the study of polytechnic, economic and legal disciplines, combined with an extensive programme of purely military sciences.

His teachers, who included prominent figures in the state and the forces, as well as respected scholars, were selected very carefully and represented a truly brilliant constellation of specialists. The role of spiritual and ideological mentor to the Tsesarevich indisputably fell to Konstantin Pobedonostsev, an expert in the law, who gave Nicholas courses in jurisprudence, public, civil

Grand Duke Tsesarevich Nicholas Alexandrovich.
St Petersburg. 1886

and criminal law. Canon law, theology, the history of the Church and of religions were presented by Proto-Presbyter Yanyshev. Ye. Zamyslovsky taught political history. Nikolai Bunge, an economics professor, minister of finance in 1881–86 and chief minister in 1887–95, taught Nicholas statistics and political economics. Nikolai Girs, Russia's foreign minister in 1882–95 introduced the Tsesarevich to the complex world of international relations in Europe. Academician Nikolai Beketov gave him a founding in general chemistry. Infantry General Genrikh Leyer, a professor and corresponding member of the Academy of Sciences, editor-in-chief of the multi-volume Encyclopaedia of Military and Naval Sciences and A Review of Russia's Wars from Peter the Great to the Present Day, was entrusted with the courses in strategy and military history. The military engineer General Cesar Cui, better known as a composer, gave lessons in fortifications. The history of the art of warfare was presented by A.K. Puzyrevsky. This venerable company also included professors from the General Staff Academy, Generals Dragomirov, Obruchev, Gudima-Levkovich, Lobko, and others.

Konstantin Pobedonostsev, Chief Procurator of the Most Holy Synod. St Petersburg. Early 20th century. Photograph by Levitsky

Konstantin Pobedonostsev (1827–1907) occupied a distinctive place among the Russian statesmen of the late nineteenth century. That place was not due to the post of Chief Procurator of the Most Holy Synod, which he held from 1880 to 1905. He has instead gone down in history primarily as the spiritual mentor and ideological guide of the last two autocrats — Alexander III and Nicholas II. Included among the teachers of both father and son, Pobedonostsev had a tremendous influence on the formation of their ideas and their view of the world (particularly in the case of the father). After Alexander II was killed by the People's Will, he remained for almost two decades the chief inspiration behind a state policy the aim of which was to preserve the established principles of the old Russia.
One of the most intelligent and educated men of his age, Pobedonostsev recognised the impossibility of stopping the onward march of time, although to the end he remained true to those principles that he had upheld all his long life. Evidently this also explains the profound pessimism that runs through his thoughts about the world around him.
As the years went on Pobedonostsev's influence on his crowned pupils gradually diminished. When the Manifesto of 17 October 1905 proclaimed the introduction in Russia of "representative government", something anathema to him (he called parliamentarism "the great lie of our age"), the mentor of two emperors realised that it was time to depart together with his era and resigned from his post. In his life Pobedonostsev made many enemies who fiercely condemned both his views and his practical activities. Yet even among those, the majority paid tribute to his rare selflessness, sincerity, intolerance of lies, and modesty verging on asceticism. He often employed his tremendous influence to help other people, some complete strangers to him, but never exploited it for his own personal benefit.

Nicholas studied a lot. By the age of fifteen he had more than thirty lessons a week, not counting the hours spent each day in preparation. Even in summer there was little change to this way of life. During the educational process his teachers were not allowed to give him marks on his progress or to ask questions in order to test his knowledge, but on the whole their impression was positive. Nicholas distinguished himself for his application, his pedantry and his innate orderliness. He always listened attentively and took his studies seriously. According to secretary of state Polovtsov, even the strict Pobedonostsev praised his abilities and worried only about the fact that the young man was "still being kept in the position of a child." Alexander III's heir, like all his children, had an excellent memory. He easily committed to mind what he heard or read. It was sufficient for him to meet a man just briefly (and there were thousands of such encounters in his life) so as to remember not only his name and patronymic, but also his age, pedigree and length of service.

Nicholas's inherent sense of tact and delicacy made dealing with him a pleasant affair. General Lobko, who lectured to the Tsesarevich on military administration, was genuinely delighted by his pupil's ability to establish "truly human, and not dry, formal relations". These qualities were overlaid with a fine education — due in no small part, it seemed to many, to the "Jesuit" Danilovich. His influence was to a considerable degree believed responsible for "that unusual restraint, which," as General Mosolov wrote, "was the main distinguishing feature of Nicholas II." Convinced that "an abundance of impressions leads to excessive distraction", Danilovich adopted a fairly rigid policy of restriction in questions of education, something that on more than one occasion provoked complaint from others no less concerned about the formation of the future ruler's character. General Gudima-Levkovich, who taught the Tsesarevich tactics, is even known to have observed on this score that Danilovich was turning his charge into "a restrained, careful old man, and not a sprightly youth". It was the feeling of many that Nicholas was not receiving enough knowledge of real life, contact with people and direct personal impressions.

NICHOLAS ROMANOV. Life and Death

Nicholas's intensive study of military subjects was combined with active service with the guards. As early as the age of seven, he was promoted to the rank of ensign and enrolled in the Life-Guards Yerevan Regiment. In subsequent years he was enrolled by turns in various guards regiments and given the next officer's rank. Nicholas was particularly thrilled when he was inducted into the glorious Preobrazhensky (Transfiguration) Regiment which at that time was commanded by his favourite uncle Grand Duke Sergei Alexandrovich. He spent two of the annual military camps in the staff of that regiment.

"I have become terribly used and fond of the service; especially those great fellows the soldiers!" he wrote in one of his letters of March 1889. "I am certain that this summertime service has been of tremendous use to me and since them I have noted great changes in myself." The heir to the throne served two more summer seasons in the Hussars and one in the artillery.

According to contemporaries, he was popular in the guards regiments who appreciated his surprisingly equable character and goodwill towards his fellow officers, irrespective of their rank or position.

The Tsesarevich was not one to be put off by the hardships of camp life. He was hardy, strong and undemanding as regards creature comforts. He also genuinely loved the army. When he first took part in major army manoeuvres near Lutsk in 1890, he delightedly informed Alexander Mikhailovich: "The troops made the kind of impression on me that I simply couldn't have imagined... The whole time the weather was cold and rainy. The terrain was difficult for manoeuvres, the length of marches enormous. Yet, despite all those adversities, at the parade all the troops presented themselves looking as, God grant, they might always remain from now on. There were 128,000 men in the formation and 468 artillery pieces, that fired a salvo as the imperial standard was raised... Every gun fired off three shots within two minutes and the whole blended with a stunning shout of hurrah! It was pleasant to see and sense that might concentrated in a small space and to realise that it was only one tenth of our entire army. My heart has rarely pounded so strongly, I can assure you."

Nicholas's military career reached its peak on 6 August 1892 when he was promoted to the rank of colonel. The premature death of Alexander III meant that his son was never destined to become a general of the Russian army as all his predecessors on the throne, and the majority of grand dukes, had been. It was not done for Emperors to give themselves military ranks.

The complete course of education for the heir to the throne ended earlier — in 1890. Shortly before his twenty-second birthday Nicholas wrote with satisfaction in his diary: "Today I ceased my studies finally and for ever." Like the absolute majority of people, he was genuinely glad to leave his student years and embark on something new, leaving what seemed the most exhausting stage in his life for one that promised to be cheerful and untroubled.

From the memoirs of Infantry General Yepanchin:
The Tsesarevich's activities were not limited to military service. Emperor Alexander III arranged that his son would be present when ministers and chief administrators reported to him. Besides, a wise rule was established that all those who were presented to the Emperor and Empress also had the right to present themselves to the Tsesarevich without making a special appointment, provided he was not busy with his service duties or his studies.
These two provisions were of exceptional importance in preparing the Tsesarevich for his future duties as ruler. He had the opportunity to make the acquaintance of many figures active in state or public service, representatives of various fields of activity, and members of different nationalities from across the extensive realm. From them he was able to learn much that was edifying, and — also a highly significant point — all these people had the opportunity to establish a personal relationship with the future Emperor.
Sadly, this rational practice was short-lived, and during the last three years of Alexander III's reign it no longer operated. In those three years the Tsesarevich's activities were indeed almost completely limited to military service; and once a week, on Mondays, he attended sessions of the State Council. I never managed to discover the reason for this change, but it is clear that it was not to the benefit of the future Tsar, rather the opposite. Those who were close to the royal family were also, so they told me, unable to determine the reasons behind such a change.

Tsesarevich Nicholas (seated in the middle) visiting the royal family in Greece. Seated second from the right in the middle row is Prince Bariatinsky. Among those standing are Prince Ukhtomsky (fourth from left), Prince Kochubei (fifth) and Prince Obolensky (tenth). 1890

Visiting King Christian IX (standing tfourth from left): Alexander III (centre, in a light-coloured suit) with Tsesarevich Nicholas behind him. Seated in the middle row: Maria Fiodorovna (second from right) with her son Mikhail, mother Queen Louise and her sister. 1889

Following a long-established tradition, the heir apparent's education culminated in a long foreign journey. As a rule, the purpose was to present the future Russian autocrat to the courts of a monarchic Europe. Alexander III chose to disregard this custom, however, and on 23 October 1890 Tsesarevich Nicholas and his brother Georgy set off on what was then an exotic voyage to the East. They were accompanied by a small retinue and joined in Athens, after two weeks, by a cousin, Prince George ("Georgie") of Greece.

The route was to take them around Asia, sailing several seas and oceans. Visits to Egypt and India were planned, to be followed by Ceylon, Singapore, Java, China and Japan. Nicholas preferred to make the return journey through Siberia, declining the tempting suggestion that he visit America, which he believed he could safely leave for some time in the future.

This voyage in a young company on close, good terms brought a lot of delights and impressions. As time went on the holds of the ships became filled with Eastern gifts and offerings — expensive fabrics, craft items, exotic fruits, drinks, and even animals. (There were elephants, a black panther, monkeys and a great many birds.) There were only two occurrences that really clouded the travellers' enjoyment — the illness of Grand Duke Georgy, who proved unable to stand the heat in India and was obliged to quit the expedition in Bombay as early as 23 January, and an unpleasant incident in the small Japanese town of Otsu that very nearly cost Nicholas his life. On 29 April the young men visited a temple and dined with the governor. As the party were boarding rickshaws to return to the ship an infuriated policeman attacked the Tsesarevich with a sabre. (One version claims that he was a religious fanatic, another a jealous madman.) He struck Nicholas a powerful blow on the head, the mark of which would always remain. Prince Georgie rushed up in time to prevent him striking again. Every year afterwards the imperial family attended a service of thanksgiving to commemorate the Tsesarevich's deliverance, but many contemporaries saw this incident as an inauspicious portent for Nicholas's future policy as a whole. While his interest in Oriental affairs never wavered, the Em-

The Russian battleship *Memory of Azov* on which Grand Duke Nicholas Alexandrowich made a round-the-world cruise. 1900s

peror clearly had no great sympathy for the Japanese, something that quite possibly affected his attitude on the eve of the armed conflict between the two countries in 1904.

On 11 May, having cut short his journey at his father's insistence, Nicholas arrived back in Russia, where "after viewing the foreign lands of the East", as Alexander III put it in his official message to him, he was to play his part in the day-to-day affairs of the state. The task that his father entrusted to him was related to the construction

During the visit to Egypt. Seated on the statue in the first row is Tsesarevich Nicholas Alexandrovich (second from left). 1890

Tsesarevich Nicholas Alexandrovich (fifth from left) during his voyage. Others include Prince Obolensky (third from right), Prince Bariatinsky (fourth), General Erikson, the crown prince of Sweden and Norway, and Prince George of Greece (seventh). Egypt. 1890

"of a railway right across the whole of Siberia that is to connect the Siberian regions with their abundant natural bounties to the network of domestic rail transportation." Tsesarevich Nicholas Alexandrovich attended the laying of the foundation stone of Vladivostok Station, to be the terminus of the great railway across Siberia.

The journey to St Petersburg — by way of Khabarovsk, Nerchinsk, Chita, Irkutsk, Tomsk, Tobolsk, Surgut, Omsk and Orenburg — took about two months. It was only on 4 August that the Tsesarevich, full of new impressions no less strong than the foreign ones, found himself back in the capital. "Think yourself, where was I to find the time in Siberia," he justified himself to Grand Duke Alexander Mikhailovich for not having written, "when even without that every day was crammed to the point of exhaustion? Despite that, I am in such raptures about what I saw that only in speaking can I convey my impressions of that rich and wonderful land, little famed up to now and (shame to say) almost unknown to us, Russians. There's nothing to be said about the future of Eastern Siberia and the South Ussuri region in particular."

In 1892 Alexander III involved the Tsesarevich in the work of the State Council and the Committee of Ministers so that he could acquaint himself directly with those highest institutions of the empire. Yet he clearly did not consider his son ready for any sort of independent role. When, at roughly this same time, Count Witte suggested naming Nicholas the chairman of the Committee for the Construction of the Eastern Siberian Railway, which would have been a customary step in the gradual engagement of the heir in current affairs of state, the Emperor was astounded and blurted out: "But he's still just a boy. His judgements are completely childish. How can he be the chairman of a committee?." At that point no-one, Alexander III included, could have imagined that the sturdy autocrat had only two more years to live.

Fate did not grant Nicholas those years close to the throne of his father during which the heirs to the Russian throne, gradually learning about affairs, mastered the difficult skills required to run the state. On the other hand it gave him an excess of something else — a rare sense of the warmth and comfort of the family that came out of his childhood, a cosiness he wanted to recreate in his own adult life. Inspired by the example of his parents, Nicholas was already dreaming of marriage when he was just twenty and felt "the need to build and establish his own little nest".

His choice fell on Alice Victoria Helen Brigitte Louise Beatrice, daughter of Grand Duke Louis IV of Hesse-Darmstadt and the British Princess Alice. After losing her mother and a younger sister at the age of six, the girl had been brought up mainly at the court of her grandmother, Queen Victoria, and spent the greater part of her childhood and youth in England. The Princess's early misfortune evidently left a mark on her. She was painfully shy and withdrawn, opening out only in the company of those closest to her, when she turned into a real *Spitzbube* — hoyden — as they called her at the German court.

Alix, as she was known, first appeared in Russia in 1884 among the relatives who came for the marriage of her elder sister Ella (Elizabeth Fiodorovna) to Grand Duke Sergei Alexandrovich. It was there that she originally met the Tsesarevich and this encounter marked the start of a childish romantic crush that subsequently grew into a stronger emotion. "Alix, Nicky" — at that time they secretly scratched their names on a window of the Italian House at Peterhof.

It is striking that in the next ten years they saw each other only twice. Their second meeting took place only in 1889, the next another five years later, in Coburg already. Between those times there were only fantasies and memories, a correspondence conducted through Ella that stoked their passions, and the disapproval of parents who were left more than cold by their son's choice.

That is not, incidentally, to imply that the Tsesarevich's heart never inclined in other directions. Back in childhood he had begun exchanging letters with Princess Victoria of Wales, whom he found increasingly attractive. "She truly is a wonderful being," he wrote to Alexander Mikhai-

Alix of Hesse. Darmstadt. 1888

lovich, "and the more and the deeper you penetrate into her soul, the clearer you see all her merits and virtues." Then, for a while Princess Olga Dolgorukaya (Dietrichstein after her marriage) entered his field of vision. After that came a long involvement — from 1890 almost to the time of his betrothal to Alix — with the rising star of the imperial theatre, the ballerina Mathilda Kschessinska. There was gossip about the relationship, but no-one in Nicholas's family ever took it seriously: the Tsesarevich was too responsible, too much a man of duty to ever link his destiny to a dancer. Alexander III took a tolerant attitude to his son's dalliance, and perhaps even hoped that Kschessinska would help him to forget the stiff German princess he and his wife disliked.

Grand Duke Tsesarevich Nicholas Alexandrovich. Livadia. 1890s

NICHOLAS ROMANOV. Life and Death

Against the expectations of his parents, who had themselves looked around for a suitable match and were inclined towards Hélène d'Orléans, the daughter of the Comte de Paris, Nicholas only became more determined.

"In the evening in Mama's rooms, three of us including Aprak [Princess Obolenskaya] discussed the family life of young society people today," he wrote in his diary for 21 December 1891. "This conversation unintentionally touched the most sensitive chord in my heart, touched on the dream and the hope by which I live from day to day. A year and a half has already gone by since I spoke to Papa about it in Peterhof, and since then nothing has changed, either for the worse or for the better. My dream is one day to marry Alix of H. I have long been in love with her, but more deeply and strongly since 1889 when she spent six weeks in Petersburg! I resisted my feelings for a long time, trying to deceive myself into believing that my cherished dream could not be realised. But when Eddy quit or was rejected [Alix turned down the suit of the son of the Duke of Edinburgh], the only hindrance or gulf between her and me is the question of religion! There is no other hurdle besides that. I am almost convinced that our feelings are mutual! Everything is in the will of God. Trusting in His mercy, I look to the future calmly and resignedly." A later conversation in which his mother spoke of Hélène of Paris placed Nicholas, by his own confession, "at a fork in the road: I myself want to go the other way, but it seems Mama wishes me to follow this one! What's to come of it?"

In those same early months of 1892 his romance with Kschessinska was blossoming ("I never thought that two identical feelings, two loves could find room in the heart at the same time," he analysed his emotions, the dream and the reality), yet the ballerina was still unable to obscure the distant and barely perceptible image of the Princess: "Now my love for Alix of H. is already into its fourth year and I constantly cherish the thought, if God grants, that one day we shall marry..."

Nicholas's choice was fully in keeping with Russian dynastic tradition. While the first Romanovs, still adhering to earlier conceptions about Moscow being "the third Rome", a holy Orthodox realm, preferred to marry girls from their own land's lesser nobility, from Peter the Great onwards the ruling house began looking to the West, primarily to Germany. Peter's son Alexis married Princess Charlotte of Wolfenbüttel, while his daughter Anna became the wife of Duke Charles Frederick of Holstein. A hundred years later Alexander I approved regulations stating that members of the Russian imperial house must only marry those of equal standing. That meant that their brides had to have been born into ruling dynasties and, since the overwhelming majority of those reigned in a Germany still fragmented into dozens of tiny states, that (together with the political calculations of the Russian autocrats with regard to central Europe) determined the pronounced German orientation for Russian dynastic marriages in the eighteenth and nineteenth centuries. Amongst the German ruling houses with the closest marital ties to the Romanov empire were those of Hesse-Darmstadt, Baden, Württemberg, Prussia and Oldenburg.
In 1762 a palace coup placed on the Russian throne the wife of Peter III, Princess Sophie of Saxe-Anhalt-Zerbst, who is better known to history as Empress Catherine the Great. Her son Paul married Wilhelmina of Hesse-Darmstadt (Natalia Alexeyevna after adopting Orthodoxy) and after her death wed Sophie of Württemberg (Maria Fiodorovna). Three of his sons took German wives: Alexander — Louise of Baden-Baden (Elizabeth Alexeyevna), Nicholas — Caroline of Prussia (Alexandra Fiodorovna) and Mikhail — Frederica Charlotte Marie of Württemberg (Yelena Pavlovna). Nicholas I's son, Alexander II, chose as his bride Princess Marie of Hesse-Darmstadt.
An exception from the "German rule" was the wedding of the future Alexander III to the Danish Princess Dagmar. Among the grand duchesses and dukes of the House of Romanov, Germany was also the preferred hunting-ground for spouses. Of Nicholas I's daughters Maria married Duke Maximilian of Leuchtenberg, Olga became the Queen of Württemberg, and Alexandra the Landgravine of Hesse-Kassel. His sons too followed tradition: Konstantin married Alexandra of Saxe-Altenburg (Alexandra Iosifovna), Mikhail — Cecilia of Baden (Olga Fiodorovna). The same thing happened in the next generation of Romanovs, although there were already more exceptions: Pavel Alexandrovich married a Greek princess, while Alexis Alexandrovich remained a bachelor.
As the twentieth century approached , although the old dynastic tradition was no longer as firm as it had been, the dense network of Russo-German marital ties still remained fairly strong.
It is no coincidence that in the official publications about the ruling houses of Europe produced abroad the Romanov dynasty was often referred to as the House of Romanov-Holstein-Gottorp, stressing its German roots.

The year 1894, which proved a turning-point in Nicholas's destiny, began with great alarm — Alexander III came down with influenza with complications as the doctors diagnosed, and for several weeks the state of his health caused his loved ones serious anxiety. Later the Emperor apparently recovered and even returned to his former way of life. Recalling this period, Sergei Witte wrote that "the sovereign himself did not acknowledge his illness. Generally, the royal family has a strange half custom, half sense of not acknowledging one's own illness and of avoiding treatment as far as possible, and this habit was particularly strongly developed in Emperor Alexander III." He attended the necessary ceremonies, stood through long church services and sat through gala dinners. Ever more obvious to those around him, though, were his paleness, puffy face, and the fact that he rapidly became fatigued.

By the summer the seriousness of his condition was obvious — chronic kidney disease as had already been precisely diagnosed brought about a sharp decline in his general state of health. From time to time the Emperor suffered from strong pains in his lower back that almost made him lose consciousness, but even in August, when the disease was at its height, he inspected the troops at their camp in Krasnoye Selo and attended the manoeuvres. Professor Zakharyin, when he arrived from Moscow, insisted on a very strict diet, a course of treatment and an urgent change of climate. He prescribed the Crimea, but Alexander, disregarding advice as usual, took his family off to Poland, to the hunting grounds of Bialowieza and then Spala.

From the memoirs of General Yepanchin:
The Emperor's personal physician was Gustav Ivanovich Hirsch, a very good man, but a doctor of the old school and hardly of the sort who should have attended His Majesty... The Emperor was built like a titan and so strong that he could bend a silver rouble with his fingers, and he considered medical aid superfluous... When analyses showed that his kidneys were not functioning properly, Hirsch took all the necessary measures. Specialists were called in and Professor Leyden summoned from Berlin... The doctors came to the conclusion that the Emperor ought to spend a certain amount of time in Egypt, or at least, on the island of Corfu.
To which the Emperor replied that, if he was destined to die, "the Russian Tsar should only die in Russia", and decided to move to Livadia.

Members of the imperial family and retainers out hunting. Seated in the first row: Grand Dukes Georgy (first from left), Nicholas (second) and Mikhail (fifth), Grand Duchess Olga. In the second row Maria Fiodorovna (third from left) and Alexander III (fourth). Poland. 1894

NICHOLAS ROMANOV. Life and Death

**From the diary
of Nicholas II:**

5 April:
Lord! What a day it has been! After coffee, about 10, we went to ... Alix's rooms. She has grown prettier to a remarkable extent, but looked exceptionally sad. They left the two of us alone and then that conversation began between us which I had long strongly desired and at the same time dreaded. We talked until 12, but with no result; she still objects to changing religion. The poor girl cried a lot. She was calmer though when we parted...

6 April:
Set off on foot with Uncle Vladimir up that same hill and got as far as the fortress itself, the keep of which has been turned into a museum of old weapons. We returned at ½ 9 and drank coffee in our shared drawing-room. Then Alix came, and she and I talked again. I touched less on yesterday's issue. It's good that she's still prepared to see me and chat...

Worsening health and the concern about the future that now depended less and less on his own will prompted the Emperor to turn his attention to questions he had long been putting off. Above all, he resolved not to hinder his children's happiness. He gave his consent to his daughter Xenia's marriage to Grand Duke Alexander Mikhailovich (Sandro), whom he evidently held in no great affection and, contrary to the general opinion of him as "a most attractive young man in all regards", believed in his heart to be a totally unsuitable match. Their marriage took place on 25 July 1894 and Alexander III, overcoming his indisposition, took part in the lengthy ritual required by court ceremonial. He also gave way to Nicholas's long-held wish, on the one hand striving to hasten his son's marriage and thus strengthen the family's future, on the other not seeing other possible brides at that time.

The matter now lay only in obtaining the consent of Alix, who had till then refused to accept Orthodoxy. It was to be resolved in Coburg during the wedding celebrations of her brother Duke Ernest Louis of Hesse and Princess Victoria Melita of Edinburgh (known as Ducky), to which the Tsesarevich was sent as head of a Romanov delegation. With him to represent the Russian Empire were three brothers of Alexander III, Grand Dukes Vladimir, Sergei (both with wives) and Pavel, Father John (Yanyshev), the royal family's chaplain, and Yekaterina Schneider, who had taught Ella Russian and, if things went as hoped, would do the same for Alix.

The possible betrothal of the Russian Tsesarevich was the subject of general interest and tense expectation that even overshadowed, as it were, the main event — the actual wedding ceremony for which members of the greatest royal houses in Europe had gathered. A part was also played in the matchmaking by the 75-year-old Queen Victoria, an acknowledged authority among the European monarchs, and by one of her numerous grandchildren — Emperor Wilhelm II of Germany.

On 8 April, the fourth day of Nicholas's stay in Coburg, after another round of persuasion, tears and agitation, Alix gave him her consent. "A wonderful, unforgettable day in my life, the day of my betrothal to my dear, darling Alix," the Tsesarevich wrote in his diary that evening. "After 10 o'clock she came to Auntie Miechen [Maria, wife of Grand Duke Vladimir] and, after a chat with her, we talked between ourselves. Lord, what a weight has slipped from my shoulders. What a joy we have succeeded in bringing to dear Papa and Mama! I have been walking around all day as if in a trance, not fully conscious of what exactly was happening to me! Wilhelm sat in the next room and waited for us to finish talking with uncles and aunts. Alix and I immediately went to the Queen and then to Aunt Marie's where the whole family were all over us for joy. After lunch we went to Aunt Marie's chapel and attended a thanksgiving service Then we all set off for Rosenau where a ball was arranged for little baby "Bee" on the occasion of her birthday! I wasn't in the mood for dancing and I walked and sat in the garden with my fiancée! I can't even believe that I have a fiancée. Came back at ¼ past 6. There was already a heap of telegrams. Dinner was at 8. We drove to see the illuminations, then went upstairs for a court concert. The Bavarian Regimental Strings played superbly. In the evening we sat together again in our drawing-room."

Grand Duchess Elizabeth Fiodorovna (1864–1918),
Elizabeth (Ella) Alexandra Louise Alice before she adopted
Orthodoxy, was the second daughter of Grand Duke Louis IV
of Hesse-Darmstadt.

Married since 1884 to Grand Duke Sergei Alexandrovich
(1857–1905), she together with her husband did much to further
the marriage of the heir to the Russian throne. For a period of
several years they did all they could to prepare for the decisive
step, not only keeping alive the mutual interest that sprang up
between Nicholas and Alix, but actively discussing the matter
with both her German relatives and the Tsesarevich.

In her own marriage Elizabeth Fiodorovna was not happy.
The couple were too different in character, they had no children
and only the profound religious sentiment they shared gave any
depth to the relationship. The spiritual gentleness and truly
Christian charity that characterised Elizabeth Fiodorovna,
enabled her to forgive Sergei Alexandrovich the many vices that
made him an unpopular figure among the House of Romanov.
The Grand Duchess found her true vocation in the sphere
of charity, caring for the poor and the unfortunate. When, after
four years of commanding the Preobrazhensky Regiment, Sergei
Alexandrovich was appointed to the responsible post of
Governor-General of Moscow, Elizabeth Fiodorovna's activities
also mainly shifted to the old capital.

Kind, charming and "exceptionally feminine in all respects",
as A.A. Polovtsov described her, she won unanimous
respect and love.

Elizabeth Fiodorovna's fine spiritual characteristics were
displayed particularly vividly after the death of her husband,
who evoked implacable hatred in all revolutionaries, at the hands
of the Social Revolutionary Ivan Kaliayev on 4 February 1905.
She not only visited her husband's murderer in prison to try to
persuade him "to repent in his heart", not only pleaded unsuccessfully on his behalf for mercy from the Tsar, but devoted
herself entirely to a selfless Christian existence.

Turning her back on social life in all its aspects, Elizabeth
Fiodorovna founded a religious house in Moscow that in 1911
became known as the Convent of SS Martha and Mary.
It was far more than just a refuge for those seeking salvation
through religion. Within the complex she established a fine
hospital by the standards of the time, a pharmacy, an orphanage
and a library. Many of the sisters went to serve in field hospitals
after the outbreak of the World War.

In April 1918 the Bolshevik authorities arrested Sergei
Alexandrovich's widow and removed her to the Urals. Detained
at Alapayevsk, some 40 miles from Yekaterinburg together with
a few other Romanovs (Grand Duke Sergei Mikhailovich, the
sons of Konstantin Konstantinovich and 17-year-old Vladimir
Pavlovich, the son of Pavel Alexandrovich) she kept all their
spirits up with her deep, genuine faith. On the night of 17 July
they were shot and thrown, many of them still living, to the
bottom of an old mine-shaft on the outskirts of Alapayevsk.

**Grand Duke Sergei Alexandrovich with Grand Duchess
Elizabeth Fiodorovna. 1884**

Grand Duchess Elizabeth Fiodorovna. 1880s

**Grand Duke Tsesarevich Nicholas Alexandrovich
with his bride Alix of Hesse. Coburg. 20 April 1894**

The happy news of the engagement delivered to Russia that same day brought a telegram in return from his parents and after a few days which Nicholas and Alix spent admiring the spring countryside at Coburg and Darmstadt, there was a personal letter from Alexander III. "My dear Nicky," his father wrote, "you can imagine with what feeling of joy and with what gratitude to the Lord we learned of your betrothal. I confess that I did not believe in the possibility of such an outcome and was sure of the complete failure of your attempt, but the Lord guided you, strengthened and blessed; and great gratitude to Him for His kindness. If you could see the joy and excitement with which everyone received this news. We immediately began getting telegrams and are still deluged with them... Now I am sure you are enjoying yourself twice as much and all you have been through, although forgotten, has I am sure been of use to you, demonstrating that not everything is obtained so easily and at no cost, and particularly such a great step that decides your whole future and all your subsequent family life! I cannot imagine you as a bridegroom. Not to be with you at such a time, not to embrace you, not to talk to you, to know nothing and to wait only for a letter with details." Agreeing that God's will was in it all, Maria Fiodorovna sincerely seconded her husband and wrote that dear Alix was already "quite like a daughter" to her and she wished that she would call her not "Auntie" as before, but "dear Mama".

Nicholas was happy. All his thoughts at this time were with his beloved fiancée. "She has so strongly changed in her attitude towards me these last days that I am brimming over with joy," he wrote. "This morning she wrote two sentences in Russian without one mistake. ... It is so unaccustomed to be able to come and go without the slightest restriction... But it is so sad to leave her, even for just one night... What sorrow to be forced to leave her for a long time; how good it was for us to be together, simply paradise."

The wedding was planned for the following spring, but as early as June, barely able to bear even that short separation, with his father's permission Nicholas set off on the yacht *Pole Star* to his beloved in England. Their idyll — marked by an exceptional openness of feelings and relations in which there were no secrets, not even the affair with Kschessinska, which Nicholas did not feel he had to hide — was full of the simplest things and unsophisticated amusements. They went walking and riding, took trips on the yacht, met relatives. In late July the Tsesarevich returned home, for the wedding of Sandro and his sister Xenia, bringing with him the happiest memories, a mass of photographs and, as always, his diary, in which Alix had written her messages for him: in English "I dreamt that I was loved, I woke and found it true and thanked God on my knees for it. True love is the gift which God has given — daily stronger, deeper, fuller, purer." "Love is caught. I have bound his wings, love. No longer will he roam or fly away. Within our 2 hearts for ever love sings." and in German "Ich bin Dein, Du bist mein, des sollst Du gewiss sein. Du bist geschlossen in meinem Herzen, Verloren ist das Schlüssellein, Du musst nur immer drinnen sein."

Members of Europe's ruling houses at Coburg. Seated in the first row: Kaiser Wilhelm II (left) and Queen Victoria (centre). In the second row: (from left) Grand Duke Nicholas Alexandrovich and Princess Alix of Hesse; (from right) Grand Duchess Elizabeth Mavrikiyevna and Grand Duchess Maria Pavlovna with the Duchess of Connaught behind her. Second from left in the third row is the Prince of Wales, the future Edward VII. At the back: Grand Duke Pavel Alexandrovich (second from left, in a bowler hat), Grand Duke Sergei Alexandrovich (centre, in a bowler and white muffler) and Grand Duke Vladimir Alexandrovich (next to him, also in a bowler) with Grand Duchess Elizabeth Fiodorovna behind. Coburg. 1894

Grand Duke Tsesarevich Nicholas Alexandrovich. 1894.
Photograph by D. Zdobnov

Princess Alix of Hesse. 1894.
Photograph by D. Zdobnov

NICHOLAS ROMANOV. Life and Death

An ominous background to the joyful expectations of the forthcoming wedding was created by Nicholas's father's rapidly worsening condition. After the Emperor again caught a chill while hunting in September 1894 the inflammatory process in his kidneys became so acute that there was no longer any hope of a recovery. When Alexander reached the Crimea his condition was practically hopeless. All the imperial family gathered at Livadia where the man who had even recently seemed the very embodiment of strength was dying an agonising death. The Tsesarevich's fiancée was urgently summoned from Germany. She arrived nine days before the Emperor's death, managed to obtain his blessing, and spent the particularly hard final days together with the others.

The death of his sincerely loved and profoundly respected father (literally in the arms of Father John of Kronstadt, a priest with a saintly reputation) was a great trial for Nicholas. The young Emperor, an exceptionally restrained individual who rarely let his feelings show, could not conceal the tears in his eyes even from outsiders. Still many years later he continued to draw mentally on the image of his father, often, according to the testimony of many, asking himself the same question — how would he have acted in this situation?

From the diary of Nicholas II:

18th October. Tuesday. A sad and painful day! Dear Papa did not sleep at all and felt so bad in the morning that they woke us and called us upstairs. What an ordeal it is. Then Papa became a little easier and dozed interruptedly through the day. I did not dare be out of the house for long... About 11 o'clock the doctors held a conference in Uncle Vladimir's rooms — it's terrible! *...19th October. Wednesday.* ...In the morning dear Papa slept continuously for four hours and sat in an armchair in the afternoon. Our worries began again towards evening when Papa moved into the bedroom and went to bed: again his weakness has become terrible! Everybody wandered about the garden separately... *20th October. Thursday.* My God, My God, what a day. The Lord has summoned our adored, dear, deeply beloved Papa to Him. My head is spinning, I don't want to believe it — the awful reality seems so unjust. We spent the whole morning upstairs by him! He had difficulty breathing and they kept having to give him oxygen to inhale. About ½ past 2 he received the Holy Sacrament; soon he began to have slight convulsions ... and the end came quickly! Father John stood by the bed for more than an hour holding his head, It was the death of a saint! O Lord, help us in these difficult days! Poor dear Mama! The requiem was held at 9.30 — in the same bedroom! I felt devastated...

Members of the imperial family in front of the palace in Livadia. 1894

The unexpected death of the Emperor was a stunning event.
"All those who needed a strong Russia," General Yepanchin
wrote about it, "were grieved and understood what a loss they
had suffered with the passing of Emperor Alexander III, while the
rest rejoiced at the disappearance of a Tsar who had given
nationalist Russia such influence." Most of all, however, the one
group and the other were scared by the uncertainty arising from
the Tsesarevich's "inconspicuousness" — what was to be? —
because up until then, as the diplomat Count Lamsdorf put it,
"the heir had not distinguished himself in any way" and was
known only by certain aspects and enthusiasms "not in the least
calculated to inspire any sort of confidence in him." Many felt
the same kind of emotions as they accompanied the late Emperor
on a last journey (much longer than those of most of his
predecessors — from Yalta to St Petersburg) that was like
a final leave-taking with the great realm that in turn paid tribute
to the monarch everywhere. The ceremonial that was strictly
observed throughout was stripped of any pomp and seemed
appropriate to the character of Alexander III. On 1 November,
having halted for a day in Moscow, the funeral train pulled into
the Nikolayevsky Station in the northern capital. From there a
slow procession made its way to the SS Peter and Paul Cathedral
where, after a week of farewells from his subjects, the Emperor
was laid to rest among his close relatives — father, mother and
elder brother.

Archpriest John of Kronstadt. Late 19th century

The funeral catafalque with the coffin of Alexander III. St Petersburg. 1894. Photograph by K.Ye. von Gan

NICHOLAS ROMANOV. Life and Death

The day after Alexander III passed away, Alix was anointed with holy oil in a ceremony attended by the immediate family to mark her conversion to Orthodoxy and adopted the name Alexandra Fiodorovna. The possibility was discussed that they should marry quietly here in Livadia "while dear Papa is still beneath the roof". The majority of the relatives rejected it. Nicholas's uncles regarded the wedding an event of state importance and insisted on a public ceremony in St Petersburg. The ceremony took place on 14 November 1894, exactly two weeks after Alexander III's funeral, on Maria Fiodorovna's birthday, when the Church allowed a little relaxation of the mourning.

The joy of the event was, of course, overshadowed by still-fresh grief, but Nicholas's long-cherished dream of starting his own family with the woman he loved had come true. "The day of my wedding!" As usual he recorded the impressions of the day gone by in his diary. "I put on Hussars uniform and at ½ 11 went to the Winter Palace with Misha. Nevsky was completely lined with troops for when Mama and Alix drove down. While they were putting the last touches to her dress in the Malachite Room, we all waited in the Arabian Room. At 10 past 12 the procession began to the great church, whence I returned a married man. My supporters were Misha, Georgie, Kirill and Sergei. In the Malachite Room we were presented with a huge silver swan from the family. After changing, Alix joined me in a coach harnessed in the Russian manner with a postillion and we drove to the Kazan Cathedral. There were swarms of people on the streets we could barely get through! On arrival at the Anichkov Palace we were met in the courtyard by an honour guard drawn from the Life-Guards Uhlans. Mama was waiting in our rooms with bread and salt."

"Who will sense it, who can express it," the young Empress Alexandra Fiodorovna wrote to her sister. *"To be in deep mourning weeping for a beloved person one day, to get married in fashionable outfits the next. There can be no greater contrast, but it is possible, it happened to the two of us... And so I have arrived in Russia, our wedding was like an extension of these funeral rites, only they dressed me in white."*

St George's Room in the Imperial Winter Palace. St Petersburg. Ca. 1903

In the haste the Emperor had not had time to prepare new apartments for himself and his bride, and the couple spent their first winter in his parents home, the Anichkov Palace, temporarily occupying the newly redecorated rooms of Nicholas and his brother Georgy. They did not have their own dining-room and usually ate together with Alexandra Fiodorovna. In the small drawing-room Nicholas received those who came to report to him; in a nearby room Alix learned Russian or replied to letters and telegrams. The cosiest place and the favourite of both was the corner room where they sat for hours, drinking coffee, reading, and so on.

Almost immediately the young pair initiated work in the Winter Palace. They visited it only a week after their wedding and, having discussed the decoration of their apartments with Ella, made the necessary arrangements. They enthusiastically talked over all sorts of possibilities, carefully "selected samples of furniture and material for the future residence ... examined various details of the furnishing of the rooms."

They looked at what their relatives were doing. By that time Xenia and Sandro had already moved into the palace — "they have done a remarkable job of decorating their apartment in the Winter Palace, what used to be the rooms of Uncles Sergei and Pavel," Nicholas noted in his diary.

Neither the Anichkov, nor the Winter Palace were to become a real home for them, however. In contrast to their predecessors, Nicholas's parents and grandparents, they preferred what Gleb Botkin (son of the court physician) described as "that charming little fairyland Tsarskoye Selo". Before 1894 was out, Nicholas and Alexandra went there twice, in November and December, enjoying some truly blissful days. They strolled through the luxurious palace halls, made themselves at home in their rooms, sorted things, went sleigh-riding all over the parks, read, slept late, looked through albums... "Each day that passes I praise the Lord and give Him thanks from the depths of my heart for the good fortune with which He has rewarded me," the Emperor wrote. "A man has no right to wish greater or better happiness on this Earth. My love and respect for dear Alix

Nicholas II with his wife Alexandra Fiodorovna. St Petersburg. 1894. Photograph by A. Pasetti

grows constantly!" The next day he added: "Words cannot describe what bliss it is to live just the two of us in such a fine place as Tsarskoye!"

As time went on his feelings for his beloved spouse only grew stronger. Anything that took him away from his dear Alix caused him unpleasant concern, trouble and distress; everything connected with her gave him a quiet sense of joy and peace. One March evening, as early as 1895, he set down what was in essence the way of life that best suited him: "We went sleigh-riding around the whole park. It was clear, but cold, and the wind even nipped our ears. After tea I wrote a letter to Mama and then read for a long time. We dined at 8. We sat in my study and I read aloud! I cannot express how I enjoy such quiet, untroubled evenings, tête-à-tête with my tenderly beloved wife! The heart of its own accord addresses a prayer of thanksgiving to God for the gift of such complete unbounded happiness on Earth."

Within the Family Circle

In the first years of his reign, the circle of people who made up Nicholas's private life remained much the same as when it formed in Alexander III's large family. The young Emperor's diary entries continually contain mentions of strolling, riding and swimming with his younger brother Mikhail, to whom he was very close in that period, as well as meetings and conversations with his beloved sisters Xenia and Olga. Xenia's husband, Sandro, was one of the most welcome guests of the imperial family, as were the Tsar's numerous uncles, cousins and second cousins. Towering above them all was the figure of the Dowager Empress Maria Fiodorovna, whose authority was generally acknowledged to be unassailable. For a long time her advice, opinions and desires retained the status of parental precepts for a son who was now the occupant of the throne.

As time went on, however, this attitude became increasingly clearly a thing of the past. Several factors played an important role in this: the nature of Nicholas's own immediate family with its tendency to look only inwards; the character of the young Empress Alexandra Fiodorovna — she failed to establish good relations with her mother-in-law, who for her part was not fond of her son's wife; and various disagreements and even family scandals with close relatives. Gradually Nicholas's day-to-day contact with people unrelated to his official duties became increasingly narrowed down to his "little family" — his adored spouse and the children, in whose company alone he felt himself truly free and easy.

Members of the House of Romanov: Grand Duke Pavel Alexandrovich (first from left), Empress Alexandra Fiodorovna (third) and Emperor Nicholas II with Grand Duke Sergei Mikhailovich behind them. From right to left: Grand Dukes Vladimir and Sergei Alexandrovich, Grand Duchesses Anastasia Nikolayevna (third) and Maria Pavlovna (fourth), with Duke George of Leuchtenberg. Tsarskoye Selo. Late 1890s

Relations between Empress Alexandra Fiodorovna and high society, including the majority of the Romanovs, ultimately boiled down to one plain fact: she was not liked. "Haughty" and "perpetually unamused", to judge by the sour, moody expression that many memoirists noted on her face, she kept herself aloof and seemed unapproachable. She was unable to make small talk or to smile as a person in her position should. The aide-de-camp Mordvinov, one of those closest to the royal couple, was among the very few who grasped that "the Empress within the circle of the family or close acquaintances and the Empress during receptions, in a company only half-familiar, were two different individuals. The former was infinitely more attractive. At home she lost her customary shyness; she joked and laughed with both the children and the guests, played a lively part in the games, and became very nimble-witted in the general conversation."

Nevertheless in the matter of the alienation of the Tsar's family from the remaining members of the imperial house she was considered the guilty party. She was also accused of exercising a baleful influence over the Emperor, who due to his supposed weakness of character was entirely under her thumb, although that too was far from the truth of the relationship that had formed between the couple.

There were few who displayed any genuine warmth of affection towards Alexandra Fiodorovna. Foremost among them was, of course,

Empress Alexandra Fiodorovna (right) and Grand Duchess Elizabeth Fiodorovna. Mid-1890-s. Photograph by K. Ye. von Gan

Grand Duke Sergei Alexandrovich, the husband of her sister Ella, together with Grand Duke Konstantin Konstantinovich, his wife Elizabeth Mavrikiyevna, and his brother Dmitry Konstantinovich, as well as Nicholas's own brother Mikhail and sister Olga.

On one of the avenues in the park at Peterhof: (left to right) Alexandra Fiodorovna, King Christian IX of Denmark, his daughter the Dowager Empress Maria Fiodorovna, Nicholas II and Grand Duchess Olga Alexandrovna. Peterhof. 1896

NICHOLAS ROMANOV. Life and Death

Grand Duke Georgi Alexandrovich. 1894

Grand Duke Georgy Alexandrovich (1871–1899)
was the third son of Alexander III and Maria Fiodorovna. His entire life was lived under the shadow of an incurable illness — a tubercular process in the lungs that was discovered while he was still very young. He began to serve in the navy, but was forced to give that up after the flare-up of the disease provoked by the abrupt change of climate during the Grand Dukes' voyage to the East in 1890–91. After 1894 Georgy was officially considered the heir to the throne and was appointed ataman (commander) of all the Cossack troops. His health did not, however, permit him to play a part in the affairs of state. Forced to spend almost all his time at his estate of Abas-Tuman high in the Caucasus mountains where conditions tended to slow the advance of the tuberculosis, the Grand Duke became interested in astronomical observations. The first high-altitude observatory in Russia was built on the estate at his expense and named in honour of its founder. After spending his final years remote from the court, Georgy Alexandrovich died at Abas-Tuman on 28 June 1899.

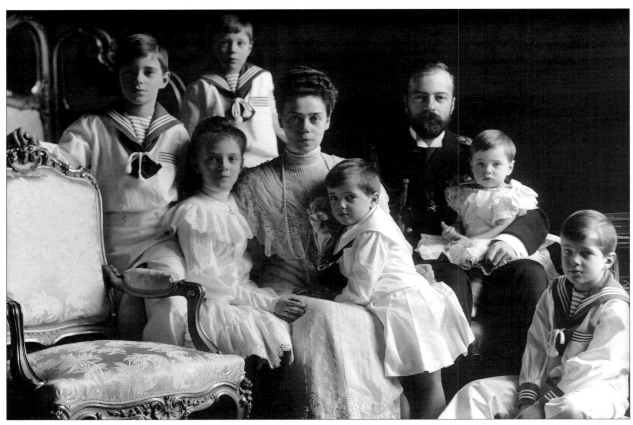

Grand Duchess Xenia Alexandrovna, her husband Grand Duke Alexander Mikhailovich and their children:
Irina, Andrei, Fiodor, Nikita, Dmitry and Rostislav. St Petersburg. 1905

Grand Duke Mikhail Alexandrovich (1878–1918),
the youngest son of Alexander III and Maria Fiodorovna, was by all accounts his parents' favourite. From 1899 to 1904 — between the death of Georgy and the birth of Alexis — Mikhail was reckoned the heir to the throne. Later he was given the title "ruler of the state" and the rights of "provisional regency" during the Tsesarevich's minority. When, however, mutual love prompted him to marry Natalia Sheremetveskaya-Mamontova-Wulfert, who had twice been divorced, it led to another scandal in the House of Romanov and Mikhail was stripped of his dynastic rights. It was only the outbreak of the First World War that allowed the couple to return to Russia, Mikhail's spouse being granted the tile Countess Brasova. The Grand Duke took command of the Caucasian Native Cavalry Division, at the head of which he distinguished himself by personal courage at the front. Relations with the Emperor's family, nevertheless, remained tense due to the open dislike that existed between the brothers' wives and Mikhail's negative attitude to Rasputin's influence. Nicholas's act of abdication on 1 March 1917 formally gave the throne to Mikhail, although as the revolution gathered pace it became impossible to occupy it. The following day Mikhail also abdicated, declaring that the future of Russia should be determined by a Constituent Assembly elected by the whole people. That move was welcomed by many, indeed one of the telegrams of approval came from exiled Bolsheviks in Eastern Siberia.

After the February Revolution Mikhail continued to live in the Gatchina Palace, but in February 1918 he was banished to Perm together with his small immediate staff by a resolution of the Petrograd Soviet. In the early hours of 13 June 1918 Mikhail and his personal secretary, an Englishman named Johnson, were taken from their rooms in the Hotel Royale by an armed group of Red Guards, driven out of the city and shot "while trying to escape".

Grand Duchess Xenia Alexandrovna (1875–1960)
belonged, together with her brothers Nicholas and Georgy, to the "older group" of Alexander III's children. She was brought up under the immediate supervision of Maria Fiodorovna, who was quite demanding, but never indulged in petty surveillance, and so was left to her own devices for a fair amount of the time. She was very close to Nicholas in childhood and adolescence. They spent their leisure hours together and shared secrets. Another childhood friend was Xenia's future husband Grand Duke Alexander Mikhailovich, a first cousin once removed known as Sandro. Their happy marriage produced seven children — six boys and a girl, Irina, who later became particularly famous for her indirect involvement in the murder of Rasputin. Sergei Witte, who knew the Grand Duchess for many years, described her as "an undoubtedly exemplary woman in all respects", of whom "it is impossible to say anything but the very best."

During the Great War she was in charge of a hospital for the wounded and took part in charitable events.

Fate spared her family in 1918. They happened to be in the Crimea and avoided the lot of the other Romanovs. In 1919 they left Russia for ever.

Dowager Empress Maria Fiodorovna with her younger children, Grand Duke Mikhail and Grand Duchess Olga. Libau. 1897. Photograph by K. Schulz

Grand Duchess Olga Alexandrovna (1882–1960),
the younger daughter of Alexander III, was the only child in the family to be born "in the purple", when her father had already come to the throne. The notable aspects of her character were simplicity, directness and geniality, which she shared with the Emperor's other children. But while the others, Nicholas above all, had to reckon with the strict demands of imperial court etiquette and subordinate their views and desires to the duties of "the first family in Russia", for her official conventions meant incomparably less. Olga Alexandrovna was very sociable, engaged wholeheartedly in charitable activities, and took an interest in art (she herself could draw splendidly). Her marriage in 1910 to the Duke of Oldenburg in North Germany proved a failure and after a few years Olga Alexandrovna left her husband and found a man who truly loved her — the guards officer Nikolai Kulikovsky. After a seven-year "trial period" imposed by Nicholas II, they married in Kiev on 4 November 1916.

During the First World War the Grand Duchess served as a nursing sister at the front and was awarded a medal for personal gallantry.

After the Revolution she left Russia together with her mother and remained with her in Denmark. As her son Tikhon recalled, Olga Alexandrovna "was in contact with the whole world, conducting an extensive correspondence... The Grand Duchess became honorary chairperson of a number of émigré organisations, mainly of a charitable kind. At that time her artistic talent was also appreciated and she began to exhibit her paintings not only in Denmark, but also in Paris, London and Berlin. A considerable portion of the money raised by this went to charity." After the Second World War Olga Alexandrovna tried to help captured Russians. This humanitarian concern was viewed with displeasure by the Soviet government that had become a threatening presence in the heart of Europe and the Grand Duchess was obliged to move to Canada where she spent her final years.

NICHOLAS ROMANOV. Life and Death

The love between Nicholas and Alexandra Fiodorovna withstood both the test of time and the numerous blows of fate. Their correspondence testifies to the astonishing depth and constancy of the emotion that bound the pair together for ever. Yet, despite the harmony of their hearts, their marriage was not destined for that complete family happiness that was the lot of Alexander III and Maria Fiodorovna. Alexandra Fiodorovna was never in good health: she had bad legs and could not ride on horseback nor play tennis or badminton which had become very popular among members of the imperial family and the St Petersburg aristocracy. The Empress found it difficult to walk and often preferred to cover even short distances by carriage. She spent much time sitting at home and on occasion, especially during her pregnancies, the doctors recommended that she restrict her movement in general. Nicholas, who since childhood was fond of physical exercise, gymnastics and walking for hours, found himself tied to his wife and quite often pushed her around the park or garden in a Bath chair. Such excursions with his beloved "other half" were perceived, incidentally, as a pleasure and not an imposition. Far more than missing out on possible amusements, the royal couple were concerned about the birth of an heir to the throne — a question of exceptional importance for any dynastic marriage.

According to the laws of the Russian Empire, the throne passed only along the male line, and therefore the birth of a son to the ruler was an absolute condition for ensuring a stable succession. Coupled with Nicholas's natural desire, shared by most men, to have a son, this created an atmosphere of tense expectation within the imperial family. Their first child, however, turned out to be a girl — Olga, whose birth on 3 November 1895 was announced to the inhabitants of the capital by a 101-gun salute. The delight of the young parents and their relatives was unbounded. "You can imagine our immense happiness: we have acquired a wonderful little one who it is so nice to care for," the Empress gushed in a letter to one of her sisters.

Disquiet and finally open alarm came later, when the Empress gave birth to one girl after another. The couple's second daughter, Tatiana, came into the world on 29 May 1897; the third, Maria, on 14 June 1899; the last, Anastasia, on 5 June 1901. They were all wanted and loved, and Alexandra Fiodorovna, who took pleasure in expending her time and energy on her children, nursed them herself. But with every year that passed the question of an heir became ever more pressing.

Nicholas II and Alexandra Fiodorovna with their daughter Olga. St Petersburg. 1896. Photograph by Levitsky

"A day I shall always remember", Nicholas II wrote on 3rd November 1895, when his first daughter was born, *"in the course of which I had much to endure! Already at one in the morning dear Alix began having pains, which would not allow her to sleep. All day she lay in bed suffering strong torments — the poor thing! I could not help feeling for her. About 2 o'clock dear Mama arrived from Gatchina; together with Ella we stayed all three of us by Alix's side. At exactly 5 o'clock we heard a baby crying and all breathed relief! God has sent us a daughter and at christening we called her Olga! When all the upset had passed and the horrors had finished, I entered a simply blessed state from what had happened! Thanks be to God, Alix came through the birth well and was in good spirits in the evening. Ate late in the evening with Mama and, when I went to bed, I fell asleep on the instant!"*

Grand Duchess Anastasia riding a donkey.
Tsarskoye Selo. 1902.
Photograph by K. Ye. von Gan

Grand Duchesses Tatiana (left) and Maria riding goats.
Tsarskoye Selo. 1902.
Photograph by K. Ye. von Gan

Nicholas II's daughters: (left to right) Grand Duchesses Anastasia and Maria (in the arms of governesses), Olga and Tatiana. 1902.
Tsarskoye Selo. 1902.
Photograph by K. Ye. von Gan

The daughters of Nicholas II: (left to right) Grand Duchesses Tatiana, Olga, Maria and Anastasia.
St Petersburg. 1905. Photograph by Boasson and Egger

The lack of a son in the imperial house created a state of dynastic uncertainty. It is interesting that after Tsesarevich Georgy Alexandrovich passed away at Abas-Tuman in June 1899, Mikhail, the youngest of the brothers, was named heir to the throne but was not awarded the title of Tsesarevich. This was the cause of talk in high social circles, especially those close to the Dowager Empress. The reason was, however, a simple one: Nicholas and Alexandra Fiodorovna hoped that they would soon produce an heir apparent. Instead, within a short time, the imperial family was plunged into a sort of dynastic crisis.

In November 1900, the Emperor, who always enjoyed astonishingly good health and toughness, fell seriously ill for perhaps the only time in his life. The doctors diagnosed typhoid, a grave, even life-threatening disease. There were moments when Nicholas's condition caused alarm. The situation was complicated because the Empress was expecting another child that might have been a boy. The illness caught the Tsar in the Crimea and an unofficial meeting was held there of senior state officials who were in the region . Sergei Witte, the minister of finance, stressed that the fundamental laws of the Empire required that in the event of the sovereign's death the throne should pass to the existing heir — Grand Duke Mikhail Alexandrovich. If after a few months the Empress should nevertheless give birth to a son, Witte stated, "only Grand Duke Mikhail Alexandrovich himself as Emperor should judge how to proceed in that event. It seems to me... he is such an honest and noble man in the highest sense of the word, that, if he considers it beneficial and just, he will himself abjure the throne in favour of his nephew."

Subsequently, it was to this very episode that Witte attributed Alexandra Fiodorovna's unwavering dislike of him. As it was, the complications that arose rapidly passed and Nicholas was soon back on his feet, while the child when it was born proved to be another girl — Grand Duchess Anastasia. Nevertheless, that episode brought home to the Empress how insecure her family's future was without a male heir. Rumours circulated that the royal couple were contemplating changing the laws on the succession along the English lines, which would mean the imperial throne passing to their eldest daughter, Olga. But the very suggestion evoked such profound disapproval, even among those as loyal to the Emperor as Pobedonostsev, that it had to be abandoned — such a decision might have provoked a deep split within the dynasty and the ruling circles with unpredictable consequences.

The Empress agonised over her inability to give her husband, and the state that he embodied, a son and heir. She sensed ever more keenly the growing undertone of hostility in court and high society spheres and began to display even more noticeably the nervous and unbalanced aspects that had always been present in her character. Alexandra Fiodorovna started to seek psychological support in religion and her faith rapidly took on a quality of mystic exaltation.

The Empress found comfort and gained hope for the birth of a son in meetings and talks with various members of the clergy, holy fools and pious wanderers (always part of the Russian spiritual tradition), who through mysterious revelations had access to higher truths.

The most striking figure among them, until the appearance of Rasputin, was Monsieur Philippe (Vachot), a native of Lyons. A wise man and spiritualist who undoubtedly possessed hypnotic powers, he was presented to the Russian royal couple during their stay in France in 1901. The following year he visited Russia several times and was received by "the first family" with exceptional trust. According to some accounts, "there was nothing remarkable about the man except his pale blue eyes, half-hidden by heavy lashes, that nonetheless sometimes flared up and gleamed with a strange softness." Philippe claimed that he could tell the sex of a child while it was still in the womb and predicted that the Empress would soon be delivered of a son. In 1902 as a consequence of his suggestions Alexandra Fiodorovna, clearly in a state of high nervous tension, even began to experience all the symptoms of pregnancy. Rumours spread widely and circles close to the court began awaiting the birth of an heir. At the end of the summer the Empress agreed to be examined by a well known specialist, the court obstetrician D.O. Ott who (as Alexander Polovtsov, a member of the State Council wrote) "immediately informed her that she was not the slightest bit pregnant... This episode did not, however, in the least shake the imperial couple's faith in Philippe, who continues in their eyes to be an excellent, inspired man." This attitude to the theurgist continued right up to his death in 1905.

Alexandra Fiodorovna also sought aid in the traditions of Russian Orthodoxy. She was especially hopeful of help from Serafim of Sarovsk, whose canonisation in 1903 was to a large extent due to the insistence of the imperial court. The decisive factor was evidently that the priest, who died in 1833 and had long been venerated by the common people, was particularly known for helping women suffering from infertility with his prayers.

According to Witte, who supposedly had the story from Pobedonostsev himself, the Chief Procurator unexpectedly received an invitation to lunch with Their Majesties "and after lunch the Emperor in the presence of the Empress announced that he wanted K.P. [Pobedonostsev] to present by the day of the feast of Serafim, which was due in a matter of weeks, a decree proclaiming Serafim of Sarovsk a saint. K.P. informed him that saints are proclaimed by the Holy Synod, after a series of investigations... At that the Empress remarked that 'the Sovereign can do anything'... The evening of the same day K.P. received a friendly note from the Emperor in which he agreed with K.P.'s argument that it could not be done at once, but at the same time he ordered that by the feast of Serafim the following year the holy man of Sarovsk be made a saint. And so it was done."

The canonisation of Serafim in July 1903 was accompanied by three days of tremendous festivities for which more than 200,000 pilgrims gathered from all corners of Russia. The Emperor participated directly in the ceremony of the translation of the new saint's relics to the Annunciation Cathedral and (unlike the other bearers who changed on the way) he carried the coffin throughout, while Alexandra Fiodorovna, despite her leg problems, stood through the almost five-hour service.

By the royal tent during the celebrations to mark the canonisation of Serafim of Sarovsk. Standing in the centre: Emperor Nicholas II, Dowager Empress Maria Fiodorovna (on his right) and Empress Alexandra Fiodorovna. 15-22 July 1903. Photograph by K. Bulla

Empress Alexandra Fiodorovna (right) and her sister Grand Duchess Elizabeth Fiodorovna going to the Chapel of St Serafim. Monastery of Sarovsk, Tambovsk province. 15-22 July 1903. Photograph by K. Bulla

Ceremonial procession with the relics of Serafim of Sarovsk during the canonisation service. The square in front of the Assumption Cathedral and Church of the Life-Giving Source, Sarovsk. 15-22 July 1903. Photograph by K. Bulla

"During this celebration," Witte continued, "there were several instances of miraculous cures. The Empress bathed at night in a spring of healing water. It is said they were sure that after four Grand Duchesses the Sarovsk saint would give Russia an heir. That came about, which finally and unconditionally planted a faith in the sainthood of the truly good holy man Serafim. A large portrait appeared in His Majesty's study — a likeness of Saint Serafim."

It is hard to say whether the intercession of the newly-created saint helped or Monsieur Philippe's prediction did indeed come true when on 30 July 1904 Alexandra Fiodorovna gave birth to her last child, the long-awaited Tsesarevich. It is not surprising that the joy of parents who had waited nine years for that day was truly boundless. "There are no words to thank God sufficiently for the comfort he has sent us in this year of difficult trials!" the happy father recorded in his diary.

They named the boy Alexis, in honour of the seventeenth-century Tsar Alexis Mikhailovich, whom Nicholas particularly esteemed. For almost two centuries a sort of taboo had existed around that name in the House of Romanov — they avoided giving it to heirs to the throne recalling the sombre tale of Tsesarevich Alexis, the son of Peter the Great, who was killed on his father's orders in 1718. Since that time the name had been considered unlucky for the dynasty. Possibly in this blatant flouting of long-established custom Nicholas was expressing his instinctive dislike for the Reformer Tsar.

General A.A. Mosolov , who was head of the secretariat at the Ministry of the Imperial Court, recalled once asking the Emperor about his attitude to the founder of the Empire, Tsar Peter I. After a short silence, Nicholas replied: "Of course, I acknowledge the many services of my forebear, but I confess that it would be insincere if I were to echo your enthusiasm. He is an ancestor whom I like less than others for his fascination with Western culture and his trampling on all the purely Russian customs. You cannot implant something foreign immediately without adaptation. Perhaps that time was indeed necessary as a transitional period, but I do not find it attractive."

**Emperor Nicholas II and his son Alexis.
Inscribed: Nicky with his son. St Petersburg. 1905**

Empress Alexandra Fiodorovna with her son Alexis. 1904

The Romanov family: (right to left) Grand Duchess Olga, Nicholas II, Alexandra Fiodorovna with Tsesarevich Alexis in her arms, Grand Duchess Tatiana; seated: Grand Duchesses Maria (left) and Anastasia. St Petersburg. 1904. Photograph by Boasson and Egger

NICHOLAS ROMANOV. Life and Death

On 11 August the Tsesarevich was baptised with all due ceremony and Nicholas recorded with satisfaction in his diary: "A momentous day... The christening began at 11. I was told later that little Alexis behaved very calmly. Olga, Tatiana , Irina and the other children first appeared in public and stood through all the long service very well indeed. Chief godmother and godfather were Mama and Uncle Alexis."

Sadly, as was almost always the case with Nicholas and his wife, the happy days with the "little treasure", as their son was affectionately known in their immediate circle, proved too short. As early as 8 September, a minor injury that could not be made to stop bleeding for a long time revealed the terrible truth — the newly-born heir to the throne suffered from haemophilia, a hereditary genetic disorder. That meant that his life was under constant threat: a scratch or slight bruise could prove fatal. A distinctive characteristic of haemophilia is that it is an exclusively male disorder — women do not suffer from it, but are the carriers who pass it on in their genes. One such carrier was the Russian Empress's glorious grandmother, the British Queen Victoria, and at that time haemophilia was sometimes referred to as "the Victorian disease". Through her the House of Hesse-Darmstadt was afflicted with this terrible legacy, something of which Alexandra Fiodorovna must have been aware. Her elder brother Frederick died of haemophilia at the age of three; her elder sister Irene, who married the Kaiser's brother, Prince Henry of Prussia, in 1888, gave birth to several haemophiliac sons.

The awareness that she was unwittingly responsible for her son's sufferings and the constant threat to his life severely affected the Empress psychologically. Despite the Tsesarevich's parents doing all they could to conceal his illness, it soon became fairly widely known in circles close to the court. The enduring antipathy towards Alexandra Fiodorovna meant that, instead of the sympathy naturally due to a mother faced with such a tragedy, she was given the blame for the degeneration of the dynasty. In high society, in the milieu of the grand dukes, they began to talk of "the inadmissible lack of care with which the choice of a bride for the heir to the throne was handled." For the imperial family difficult years, full of tension and alarm lay ahead.

A complete end was put to all the social amusements, tremendous receptions and festivities of earlier times. The splendid court balls, adorned by all the senior nobility of the Empire, became a thing of the past. From now on there were only purely official celebrations and events dictated by protocol, and the Empress attended even those fairly rarely. The life of the royal family became even more secluded, hidden from outside eyes, visible only to a few.

Nicholas loved his son beyond measure and shared his wife's disquiet. In a certain sense his position was even harder: his alarm over Alexis was made heavier by alarm about the Empress herself, whose psychological health became increasingly a matter for concern as the years went on. Nicholas bore his cross with truly Christian humility. His endurance and dignity were supported by a deep and genuine faith, the like of which was probably not possessed by any of his crowned predecessors.

The documentary book The Murder of the Russian Imperial Family, published in Paris in 1925 (its author, Nikolai Sokolov, was a former legal investigator for the Omsk circuit court and had in March 1919 been entrusted by the White leader Admiral Kolchak with discovering the facts surrounding the killing of Nicholas II, his family and other members of the house of Romanov in the Urals), includes testimony by Mrs Zanotti, a former lady-in-waiting at the Russian Court, who was very close to and fond of the Empress and had been at her side practically all the time. According to her evidence: "The Tsarina was suffering, it seems to me, from hysteria. In the last years she was not the same as she had been earlier... What it was that fuelled the Empress's hysteria, I can't tell you... Doctor Dranitsyn and Doctor Fischer who treated the Empress might tell you that... A few years ago the Empress was complaining of her heart, went to Nauheim and consulted Doctor Grotte. Grotte did not find any heart disease. It seems to me, he discovered some nervous disorders and insisted on a completely different regimen. Fischer then found the same thing with Her Majesty. He even made a secret report to the Emperor about the Empress's illness. Fischer predicted with exact precision what would then begin to happen with the Tsarina. In particular he indicated treatment not of her heart which was evidently healthy, but of the nervous system. But the Empress found out about Fischer's report. He was dismissed and Botkin was summoned."

The court Church of the Holy Apostles Peter and Paul in the Great Peterhof Palace where Tsesarevich Alexis was baptised. Peterhof. 1900s. Photograph by K. Bulla

From Anna Vyrubova's book *Unpublished Memoirs:*

The little heir occupies a special place in my recollections.
At first he was a pretty boy, physically well developed and his mother would say with pride that the birth had been easy too.
Soon, though, it turned out that the child was far from healthy.
A medical examination showed internal bleeding. At first they thought that it was merely something temporary, but soon the doctors established that the Tsesarevich had a terrible incurable hereditary disease — haemophilia. Women do not suffer from that disease, but they pass it on from generation to generation to male descendants.

Even the healthy blood of the Romanovs — for the Romanovs are in general a strong, healthy stock — could not overcome this inherited disorder and it afflicted the heir to the throne...

The Tsesarevich's illness was a terrible blow to the Emperor and Empress. I am not exaggerating if I say that the sorrow undermined the Empress's health. She could never rid herself of a feeling of responsibility for her son's illness. The Emperor himself aged many years in just one and those who observed him closely could not but noticed that he was constantly troubled by alarming thoughts.

I remember a beautiful child, like a cherub, with golden hair and delightful intelligent eyes; but at the slightest knock his body became covered in bruises. They protected the heir as best they could, but it was far from always effective. He was an active child and after every knock he would cry bitterly for nights on end.
I remember how the Empress worried when they were expecting some eminent foreign guest and how she strove to have the Tsesarevich looking healthy. At first they kept the disease a secret — everyone hoped he would get over it.
Once, on the eve of the Kaiser's arrival, no amount of safety measures helped: the boy fell and a large bruise appeared on his forehead. The Kaiser, of course, immediately grasped what was wrong with the boy, as two or three of his brother Prince Henry's sons suffered from the same disorder.

We who were close to the Empress were plunged into deep sorrow observing her growing melancholy. Even earlier she had been shy and withdrawn, even at times seemingly unhappy. Now, though, all those features of her character emerged even more strongly. The war with Japan and its gloomy consequences could not have lightened the Empress's concerns.

Her health grew worse; she continually felt tired and ill and only an enormous effort of will enabled her to conceal her maladies for years on end so that they did not become known even in court circles.

For the first year the Empress concealed her son's illness even from me. I found out about it by chance. Once — in Tsarskoye Selo, it was — the Empress and I were playing the piano four-handed. The Tsesarevich was sitting alongside us on a folding chair and a table like little children usually have. Someone came in unexpectedly and the Empress left me with the boy.
I got up so as to take him in my arms, but he immediately began crying and then screamed like a little wounded animal.
The Empress came running and shouted: "Leave him, stop, his leg's caught in the chair!" I could not understand what the matter was. "I'll explain in a minute," the Empress said.
Little by little she managed to quiet her son, but I noticed that the Tsesarevich's leg was bruised and swollen.
The Tsarina in tears told me about the dreadful disease.
The Emperor's health did not suffer and he sought consolation in work. He was busy from morn to night, often not going to bed before one.

NICHOLAS ROMANOV. Life and Death

From Vladimir Gurko's book *The Tsar and Tsarina:*

While Alexandra Fiodorovna's reason was sometimes fuddled by her runaway passion, while her decisions were fatally influenced by her inherent high-handedness and self-assurance, nonetheless the chief reason for those profound errors into which she fell in the last years of Nicholas II's reign was another side of her psychological make-up, that with the years acquired ever greater power over her and little by little turned into what was definitely a morbid condition — her all-penetrating, deep-running mysticism.

Members of the House of Hesse to which the Empress belonged had been prone to mysticism for ages, over many generations... The Empress's sister, Grand Duchess Elizabeth Fiodorovna, was also full of religiosity, running to mysticism. In Alexandra Fiodorovna deep religiosity was present from youth, finding outward expression, among other things, in her spending hours kneeling at prayer.

Inspired by that same religiosity, before her wedding she accepted Orthodoxy with all her being. This did not prove a difficult task for her: in Orthodoxy she found abundant nourishment for her innate inclination towards the mysterious and the miraculous.

It is there that we should seek the explanation for her resolve to change her faith, something which, it emerges from the Emperor's diary, she was originally against. Sure enough, Alexandra Fiodorovna, having adopted Orthodoxy, did not regard it with anything like the relative indifference that the Russian educated public had shown since the 1870s. She, on the contrary, absorbed Orthodoxy with all her being, and Orthodoxy roughly sixteenth-century style at that. She acquired a profound belief not only in all the dogma of Orthodoxy, but also in all its ritual aspect. In particular, she became imbued with a profound faith in the saints venerated by the Orthodox Church. She zealously placed candles before their images and finally, and this is most important, became imbued with a faith in "men of God" — hermits, monks of the strictest rule, holy fools and soothsayers. The Empress strove to establish contacts with people of this kind from the earliest years of her life in Russia and individuals appeared who provided her with them in such numbers that the royal palace in that respect acquired the character of the old-world homes of Moscow's rich merchants. Using the back entrance, of course, at someone or other's recommendation such people penetrated into the inner apartments of the palace, where the Empress talked with them sometimes at length, while the household staff were expected to cordially treat them to food and drink.

The Tsarina even said on this account that she was aware of the reproaches cast at her because she liked to see and talk with wandering pilgrims and various "men of God". "But," she added, "such people speak much more strongly to my mind and heart than the Church hierarchs who come to me in expensive silk vestments. So, when I see a metropolitan coming in to see me, his silk robe rustling, I ask myself: what's the difference between him and elegant high-society ladies?"

At the same time she immersed herself in the written works of the Church Fathers. Those tomes were her preferred reading to such an extent that alongside the couch, on which she spent the greater part of her time, stood a book-stand containing a large number of books with a religious content. The majority of these books were not only Russian, but written in Church Slavonic, which the Empress learned to understand readily.

Her favourite activity, like the Russian Tsarinas of the time before Peter the Great, was embroidering items of ecclesiastical linen. The idea sprang up owing to the spirit of the Orthodox faith and then became fixed in her mind that the salt of the earth in Russia were the common people, while the higher classes were corroded by lack of faith and marked by depravity. Another factor

played an immense, decisive role in strengthening this view in her, colouring in a most particular way, that became ever stronger with the years, her attitude to the various sections of the Russian populace. I refer to the circumstances in which she found herself on her arrival in Russia, which almost coincided with her assuming the role of empress consort, that is to say the reception that she encountered from some members of the imperial family and also many prominent members of St Petersburg society. Her every word, every gesture, everything down to the cut of the dress she was wearing was subjected to harsh criticism; and obliging people came forward who made sure she knew about it... Naturally, little by little, not by any means at once, Alexandra Fiodorovna also began to harbour unkind thoughts about St Petersburg society and therein lies one of the reasons, if not the main reason, why she turned to the Russian popular masses and sought from them the sympathy that the St Petersburg nobility had not shown her. Moreover, because of this the Empress developed a mistrust towards people that with time acquired a certain morbid character. Almost a majority of the royal family and of society turned in her eyes into her personal insidious enemies. The slightest criticism of her words and actions, or even a failure to acknowledge her absolute wisdom, were to her mind an irrefutable sign of hostility towards her. How great the trust, how great the sympathy enjoyed by those who agreed with her propositions, praised her decisions and skilfully expressed boundless devotion to her. Under this same influence the Empress developed a susceptibility to flattery. There can be no doubt that the Empress's confidence in the unshakeable firmness of the autocratic system in Russia was founded on the conviction that the common people, the Russian peasantry worshipped their monarch.

The St Theodore Cathedral of His Imperial Majesty's Own Escort and His Imperial Majesty's Own Regiment of Foot (built 1910–12, architect Vladimir Pokrovsky). Tsarskoye Selo. 10 February 1912. Photograph by K.K. Bulla

Constructed in a purely Russian style, the St Theodore Cathedral in Tsarskoye Selo was erected on the initiative and the funds of Alexandra Fiodorovna.. "Equipped and decorated through her personal care and totally by her direct choice," as Count V.N. Kokovtsov wrote, this church gave her the calm and repose she sought. "She came there, most often alone, at the times of services, sometimes at other times, and there she gave herself up to her truly prayerful mood without any intercourse with the world. There her belief in all things miraculous strengthened, and it was thither that she withdrew each time when she was seized by all manner of doubts or cares, and the complications of life pierced deep into her soul."

NICHOLAS ROMANOV. Life and Death

Compared to the religious obsession of Alexandra Fiodorovna, the Emperor's faith was much calmer, lacking her exaltation. In Nicholas it combined naturally with an unwavering devotion to all things Russian, to traditions that went back into the depths of the centuries. The outward expression of this was the dislike of Peter the Great that has already been mentioned and a clear preference for the legacy of old Muscovy. This preference made itself felt in literally everything: in Nicholas's reign the "Neo-Russian" style that drew on the traditions of construction before Peter the Great began to dominate in public architecture, especially places of worship; many archaic rituals were revived in court ceremonial, particularly in religious contexts. There were even plans to replace the uniforms of all those who served at court, from footmen and cooks to high officials, who, it was proposed, would wear Russian seventeenth-century costume. This idea had to be abandoned due to the tremendous expense involved in its implementation, but the Emperor's taste for the traditional dress of his ancestors found an outlet in more modest undertakings — the fancy-dress balls of the early years of the twentieth century, the last great balls at the imperial court.

It is well known that the Emperor disliked the use of foreign words in official state documents. "The Russian language is so rich," he commented on one occasion to General Mosolov, "that it permits the substitution of Russian expressions for foreign ones in all instances. Not one word of non-Slavonic origin should disfigure our language... I underline all the foreign words in a report with a red pencil. Only the Ministry of Foreign Affairs does not succumb to the pressure and continues to be incorrigible."

The same loyalty to national traditions characterised Nicholas's everyday life, his tastes and habits, making itself felt at times even in trivial matters. "Like his father, Emperor Alexander III," the aide-de-camp Mordvinov recollected, "Tsar Nicholas Alexandrovich was not fond of clothing that restricted his movement and preferred in his domestic life old clothing, that was well-worn and as a result much mended. When people came to see him he received them in his study, also dressed with complete simplicity — either in a grey double-breasted jacket or sometimes in the crimson silk shirt of the Imperial Family's Fusiliers, of which he was very fond because it was not only comfortable, but also national, Russian. During the war he invariably wore a very unattractive khaki shirt of coarse, thick soldier's cloth and a soldier's greatcoat of the same kind."

Modest and unpretentious (like, incidentally, the other members of his family), Nicholas was also very restrained in his eating habits, and preferred plain Russian dishes to all kinds of delicacies. Refined culinary works of art were served only at official court dinners and celebrations.

There was, however, a dangerous political aspect to the Emperor's attachment to all things truly Russian. He was deeply and sincerely convinced that autocratic power was as much a pillar of national existence from time immemorial as the Orthodox faith. In his eyes the triad encapsulated in the slogan "Orthodoxy, Autocracy and National Character" was a reality replete with profound meaning. From that sprang the Emperor's unwavering conviction that despite political shocks the people — and above all the country's many million peasants — continued to remain loyal to the throne, because that was inseparable from loyalty to the Motherland. That conviction was not destroyed even by the collapse of the monarchy and the revolutions of 1917. Nicholas and Alexandra Fiodorovna left this life in the certainty that everything that was happening was darkness and delusion, that the nation had simply gone astray, the way people fall into sin, while in the depths of its heart the sacred flame of monarchist feeling still burned. In the final analysis that belief proved fateful for the dynasty and the monarchy.

Emperor Nicholas II in fancy dress. 1903

Under the Burden of Power

Among the masses the beginning of the new reign was met if not with enthusiasm then at least with great hopes and expectations. Faith in the monarch was still unshaken. The underlying public attitude consisted of dreams that Russian life, "frozen" during the reign of Alexander III, would become more lively. Recalling these years later General Alexei Ignatyev, then a page to the Empress, defined the public mood quite well: "No-one had any dark premonitions in that winter of 1895/96," he wrote. "We all keenly anticipated the best from the new young Emperor and took delight in his every gesture, seeing in this if not the start of a new era, then at any event the breaking down of the Gatchina existence established by Alexander III.

"The Tsar moved his residence to sunny, gay Tsarskoye Selo. The Tsar opened the rusted doors of the Winter Palace. The young couple without any guard simply rode about the capital in a sleigh. And even the statement about 'impossible dreams' that the Tsar made during a reception for the Tver nobility was perceived as a temporary misunderstanding."

The first gloomy omen for the new reign was the well-known disaster at Khodynka Field that took place in May 1896 during the coronation celebrations. It was this ominously symbolic event that became for Nicholas the beginning of a long series of personal, family and national tragedies and failures that with a dreadful inevitability led the age-old monarchy and its last ruler to a fatal end.

There was naturally, in nearly all cases, a gap in time between the succession of a new monarch and the coronation ritual in the old capital, Moscow, with its accompanying celebrations. The length of the interval varied and depended on a number of factors, but above all on the wishes of the new Emperor. Usually the coronation was timed for spring or summer as the people traditionally celebrated outdoors. On this occasion it was to take place in mid-May.

The Romanov family during the coronation festivities: standing (left to right) Grand Duke Kirill Vladimirovich, Nicholas II, Grand Duke Sergei Alexandrovich, Grand Duchess Victoria Melita of Hesse-Darmstadt; seated in the middle row (right to left) Grand Duchess Elizabeth Fiodorovna, Grand Duchess Elizabeth Mavrikiyevna with her son Igor, Empress Alexandra Fiodorovna with Grand Duchess Olga. Seated on the carpet is Grand Duke Pavel Alexandrovich and (to his right) his daughter Grand Duchess Maria. Moscow. 1896

Panorama of Moscow. Late nineteenth century

A special coronation commission was set up under the Emperor's uncle, Grand Duke Sergei Alexandrovich and including Ilarion Vorontsov-Dashkov, the Minister of the Imperial Court and Domains, Vladimir Fredericks, his deputy and the Chief Master-of-Ceremonies Konstantin von der Palen. This commission drew up an extremely detailed programme for the coronation celebrations.

"Long before the appointed day, guests from all parts began gathering in Moscow, the ancient capital," the historian S.S. Oldenburg wrote, reconstructing the chronicle of events. "Every day brought new spectacles: at times the arrival of foreign ambassadorial delegations; at others military parades... The Russian coronation celebrations of 1896 were, incidentally, the first major state festivities to remain recorded on cinematographic film (in April 1897, at the Salt Town in St Petersburg "living photographs" (19 pictures by the Lumieres) were shown for the first time.) The newspapers listed the exalted guests: the Queen of the Hellenes, Olga Konstantinovna, had come; Prince Henry of Prussia, the brother of Wilhelm II; the Duke of Connaught, a son of the British Queen; the Italian Crown Prince Victor Emmanuel; Prince Ferdinand of Bulgaria; Prince Nicholas of Montenegro; the Greek Crown Prince Constantine; the Romanian Crown Prince Ferdinand; German grand dukes and princes. According to *Novoye Vremya* the coronation was attended by: one queen, three grand dukes, two ruling princes, twelve crown princes, sixteen princes and princessess...

A prominent place in the festivities was also taken by the Chinese delegation led by Lee Hun Chan." The number of representatives from Eastern nations was also considerably greater that at the previous coronation in 1883. For the first time there were envoys of the Patriarchs of Constantinople, Antioch, Jerusalem and Alexandria, of the Vatican and the Anglican Church.

The visitors arriving daily in Moscow completely changed the look of the city. Journalists wrote that it was as if the entire population had been replaced. A rich mix of national facial types and costumes speaking a variety of languages filled the streets so that in some places particularly prone to jams of all manner of conveyances "you had to wait hours on end to cross from one side to the other."

Members of the Vatican delegation. Standing (left to right) Count Marino Salluzzo, the Duke de Corigliano and Count Mario Carpegna; seated Genarro Granito de Belmonte, the papal nuncio Aliardi, ambassador extraordinary Ferdinand de'Cron and Francesco Tarnassi. Moscow. 1896

Crown Prince Frederick of Denmark with his retinue. Seated (left to right) General Engelbrecht, the Crown Prince, and Adjutant-General Admiral Kremer. Standing (left to right) aide-de-camp Prince Bariatinsky, Colonel Bull and Captain de Kefed-Hansen. Moscow. 1896

The emotional charge of the ceremony was tremendous. "The service did not exhaust me in the least, but rather inspired me with the awareness that I am entering into a mystic marriage with Russia," Alexandra Fiodorovna wrote to her sister Victoria. *"Now I am truly the Tsarina."*

Members of the British delegation: standing (left to right) Count Ribopier, Colonel Edgerton, Admiral Fullerton, Colonel Welby, General Grenfell, Captain Lord Bingham, Cavalry-Captain Prince Kuchubei, Colonel Water and Sotnik Orlov; seated (left to right) lady Edgerton, General Prince Golitsyn, the Duchess and Duke of Connaught. Moscow. 1896

Governor-General of Moscow, Grand Duke Sergei Alexandrovich, organiser of the coronation celebrations (centre right) with Grand Duke Pavel Alexandrovich next to him. 15 May 1896

Nicholas II, in the royal mantle with crown, sceptre and staff, processing beneath the baldachin in the Kremlin. Moscow. 14 May 1896

The coronation ceremony took place on 14 May, "a great, festive day, yet hard in a moral sense", as Nicholas described it. "All this took place in the Assumption Cathedral, although it really seems like a dream, the memory of it will last a lifetime!!!" He recognised in full measure the significance of a rite whose roots went back into the depths of time. Until he was anointed with holy oil, the monarch was not considered to have come to power completely — only the Church through its senior clergy could give the Emperor ultimate authority.

The entire ceremony lasted about four hours. The service was conducted by Pallady, the Metropolitan of St Petersburg, with many other high clergymen in attendance. The Emperor recited the Creed, as required, then he was enrobed. Wearing the crown and holding the orb and sceptre, he pronounced the coronation prayer and listened to the response spoken by the Metropolitan on behalf of the people. After the liturgy Nicholas was anointed with holy chrism, made his oath, and — for the first and last time in his life — entered the sanctuary to take communion "by the royal rite". As he ascended the steps the chain holding the Order of St Andrew the First-Called slipped from his shoulders. This was seen only by those close by and for fear of unfavourable gossip the occurrence was hushed up.

NICHOLAS ROMANOV. Life and Death

The tragedy that overshadowed all other events took place on 18 May. At Khodynka Field out to the north-west of the city dozens of buffets and pavilions had been constructed. At 10 o'clock the programme called for the distribution of royal gifts — 400,000 packages of food and enamel mugs decorated with the Tsar's monogram, to be followed by theatrical performances and, at 2 p.m., a royal appearance. People began gathering the evening before, evidently motivated by the thoughts later expresses by the workman Vasily Krasov. "To wait until morning so as to come for ten o'clock, the time appointed for the distribution of gifts and commemorative mugs, seemed plain stupid to me," he recalled. " With so many people there'd be nothing left when I arrived in the morning. And am I going to live to see another coronation?.. To be left without a reminder of such a celebration seemed to me — as a Muscovite through and through — a disgrace: was I to be like some corner of a field they'd forgot to sow? They said the mugs were very pretty and would 'last forever'... Back then enamel cups and things were a real marvel..."

Khodynka Field was used as a military training ground and dotted with ditches and trenches. It had not been prepared for events of this kind. The catastrophe came at about six in the morning. The crowd, responding to rumours that some people were already enjoying their presents, started to stir, "suddenly shifted like a single person and hurled itself forward with such haste as if it was being chased by fire," one eye-witness testified. "The back rows pressed against the front ones. If someone fell they were trampled by people who had lost the ability to tell that they were walking over bodies still alive as if over stones or logs." At 8 o'clock news of the disaster reached the Governor-General, Grand Duke Sergei Alexandrovich, and soon after the stunned Emperor knew: "A great sin has occurred," he wrote in his diary. "The crowd that had spent the night on Khodynka Fiekd awaiting the start of the distribution of meals and mugs pressed towards the stands and a crush took place there in which, terrible to add, about 1,300 people were trampled!!" Even according to the official statistics alone, 2,690 people fell victim to the incident, 1,389 of them lost their lives. The subsequent enquiry attributed responsibility to the Moscow police and the Governor-General who became known among the common people as "Prince of Khodynka". Vlasovsky, the head of the police, was dismissed. Those fortunate enough to survive that night outside Moscow recalled "Bloody Saturday" as one of the worst experiences of their lives.

Popular festivities on Red Square. Moscow. May 1896.
Photograph by Bychkov and Zhdanov

According to the future Minister of Foreign Affairs, Alexander Izvolsky, the imperial couple were deeply affected by the catastrophe. "The Emperor's first impulse was to stop the festivities and to withdraw to a monastery," he wrote. "His uncles persuaded him not to cancel anything, in order to avoid an even greater scandal. Maria Fiodorovna on the contrary insisted on cancelling all amusements.

Even on the very day of the tragedy, the festivities on Khodynka Field, the special performance in the Bolshoi Theatre and the ball at the residence of the French ambassador, Count Montebello took place without any amendments to the programme.

Although, as the British ambassador testified, the Empress appeared at Count Montebello's residence in great distress, her eyes red from tears, the evening in general left a bad after-taste. The political motivation — Nicholas did not wish to cast a shadow on this expansive gesture of French affection for Russia — was not comprehensible for the majority of the population. "The festival on top of the corpses" the noted reporter Vladimir Giliarovsky dubbed the train of celebrations in which banquet followed banquet, formal dinners alternated with grand receptions and balls almost every night — at the Governor-General's, in the Noble Assembly, the Alexandrovskaya Hall...

In the days immediately after Khodynka, Nicholas and Alexandra travelled around the hospitals, witnessing terrible sights and comforting the victims, and also attended the requiem service. The sum of 1,000 roubles was allotted to the families of the dead and injured. All the funeral expenses — the bodies each in a separate coffin and not in a common grave as often happened with disasters — were met by the state. At the Tsar's own instruction a special orphanage was founded for children who had lost their parents. "No attempt was made to conceal or diminish what had occurred," S. Oldenburg wrote. "Reports of the tragedy appeared in the papers the very next day, 19 May, to the surprise of the Chinese envoy Lee Hun Chan, who told Witte that far from being published such sad news should not even have been conveyed to the Emperor!... Public opinion began to seek out the guilty. Left-wing publications alluded to 'the general conditions' and wrote, among other things, that if the people had more sensible diversions, they would not have been so greedy to get the presents..."

The reputation of the Emperor, who from that point on was referred to ever more often as "Nicholas the Bloody", was considerably tarnished and even the manifesto granting all manner of benefits to those affected (as was usual in such cases) did not improve the general negative impression.

Having at last reached the end of a very draining three weeks, Nicholas wrote in his diary with an enormous feeling of relief on 26 May: "Thank God, the last day has come!" After a glittering military parade, held on that same ill-starred Khodynka Field, a farewell reception for the foreign delegations, and a large dinner for the Moscow authorities and representatives of the different estates, the royal couple left the old capital. The following morning, at Ilyinskoye, the estate outside Moscow belonging to Grand Duke Sergei Alexandrovich and Elizabeth Fiodorovna, Nicholas and Alexandra "woke up with the wonderful awareness that everything was over, and now we can live for ourselves quietly and peacefully!"

They were still happily ignorant of the fact that recent events were only the start of a long and difficult road, full of trials. The hardest times still lay ahead.

NICHOLAS ROMANOV. Life and Death

Nicholas came to power in a period of deep calm at home and enduring peace in Europe. The country's economy was developing at a hitherto unseen pace and Russia's established appearance was changing by the day. Factories sprang up on what had only recently been agricultural land on the outskirts of cities; a network of railways spread to more and more new industrial regions, mines and ports. In a mere decade the length of the Empire's railways and its industrial output both doubled. In metallurgy and machine-building the figures tripled. The "colossal wealth of the country", first shown in all its scope at the 1896 exhibition in Nizhny Novgorod, was truly striking.

The Russian ship of state continued by inertia to follow the course established by Alexander III, who with a firm hand put an end to the "sedition" and terrorist outrages of the late 1870s and loudly declared his will in domestic and international affairs. The outwardly indisputable prosperity of the first years of Nicholas's reign was a direct continuation of that period, but even then many more far-sighted people noted with disquiet the gradually multiplying signs that beneath the surface things were not well with the established order in the Empire, for all that it still seemed indestructible. From the very start of his rule Nicholas encountered many serious problems that grew ever more from year to year.

The new Emperor inherited unbridled power, but not his father's masterful nature and authority. Alexander III was able to engender respect even among his enemies and those who wished him ill, not to mention the assistants he himself appointed. The Emperor was noted for a crude directness in his relations with those around him, not shrinking from expressing harsh, at times quite frank opinions of people who had incurred his displeasure in some way.

Nicholas, by contrast, "did not possess the commanding character proper in a ruler." One of the most perspicacious contemporaries, who has left us perhaps the best psychological portrait of the last monarch, Vladimir Gurko wrote that "he completely lacked that inner power that subjugates people, forcing them to obey unquestioningly. The chief characteristic of a popular leader — a masterful authoritative personality —

the Emperor did not have at all. He himself sensed this; the whole country instinctively sensed it, still more those who had direct contacts with him."

It is remarkable that the beginning of Nicholas's reign was not marked by something characteristic of a change of power under any authoritarian regime — the appointment of new people. Almost all the existing ministers remained at their posts; the grand dukes, who had been left in the shadows, became noticeably more active and increased their influence. Particularly forceful were his uncles Sergei Alexandrovich and Alexander Mikhailovich. "Having sat quietly while Alexander III was alive, the grand dukes now made their voices heard loudly and without restraint," recalled V. Krivenko who served in the Ministry of the Imperial Court for many years. "Vladimir Alexandrovich did not interfere in domestic policy, but advanced himself well to the fore in the sphere of external representation. Sergei Alexandrovich became a particularly close advisor, a representative of the Muscovite conservative party. Nikolai Nikolayevich began to gather the threads of military administration in his hands; and after him, somewhat later, a new claimant to power appeared — Sergei Mikhailovich who managed to resurrect if not the title, then the traditions of the General-Feldzechmeister [head of artillery]. The appearance in the arena of state affairs of this group of irresponsible figures ... heralded nothing good for the future."

The grand dukes were very different characters and at times openly at loggerheads with each other. Vladimir Alexandrovich and Maria Pavlovna, who were the heads of the next most senior branch of the House of Romanov, clearly aspired to a special position at court, although many disliked their family for its inherent arrogance and presumption. Alexander Mikhailovich took a strongly negative attitude to the influence of "Uncle Sergei". Sergei Alexandrovich in turn regarded Alexander Mikhailovich and Konstantin Konstantinovich as dangerous liberals, advised the Emperor not to listen to "the harmful advice of Kostya and Sandro". There were also sharp clashes between Alexander Mikhailovich and Admiral-General Alexei Alexandrovich.

Members of the House of Romanov: Emperor Nicholas II (fourth from left), Grand Dukes Vladimir Alexandrovich (first), Pavel Alexandrovich (fifth) and Piotr Nikolayevich (sixth); (on the balcony) Grand Duke Mikhail Nikolayevich, Grand Duchess Maria Pavlovna and her daughter Elena Vladimirovna. Ropsha. 31 July 1899

Nonetheless, the main problem for the Emperor proved to be not his relations with the grand dukes but the need to take decisions personally in affairs of state. Like any authoritarian regime, autocracy required for its political effectiveness a single will that united and directed all. Without that, state power, broken up into separate, mutually independent institutions not controlled by society, could only go with the current of events. After the death of Alexander III, who held the whole unwieldy mechanism of state under his control, a breakdown in its established operating routine began to show. In December 1894 the former state secretary Polovtsov noted in his diary that with the change of reign the ministers had ceased to submit their proposals to the State Council, evidently waiting for the new direction of policy to be determined. This Russian peculiarity placed a heavy burden on the Emperor, requiring him to display not only diligence and strength of character, but a wide range of other abilities besides.

Nicholas was conscientious in the extreme regarding his duties. He personally acquainted himself with the contents of all the papers delivered to him — like his predecessors he never had either secretaries or abstracters. Ministers, diplomats, senior military and civil officials were received as regularly as before. But Nicholas's approach to the use of his power was limited in character. He preferred to examine specific matters as and when they cropped up. Given such a view, the business of ruling was to a large extent reduced to making resolutions on the papers he received. The Emperor was reacting to events and in his position there was more than ever a need to be ahead of them, to direct their development with his decisions.

At the same time Nicholas had an extremely exaggerated conception of the extent of his power and its possibilities. That perhaps goes a long way to explaining the fact, paradoxical at first sight, that it was psychologically easier for him to abdicate, to lay down the burden of autocracy altogether, than to accept any restriction on it, even the slightest. His decisive rejection of the very idea of the public being involved even in the simple discussion of the affairs of state emerged clearly in the very first months of his reign.

NICHOLAS ROMANOV. Life and Death

Nicholas II with his entourage accompanying the carriage of Empresses Alexandra Fiodorovna and Maria Fiodorovna. St Petersburg. 2 May 1903

On 17 January 1895, while receiving deputations of the *zemstva* (elected district councils) from the provinces following his succession, Nicholas abruptly dismissed the very timid wishes for "the right to express our opinion" contained in the address of the men from Tver province. The Emperor called them "impossible dreams", which immediately caused a large and on the whole hostile response among the public, who were clearly disappointed in their hopes for liberalism from the new monarch.

As he spurned any chance of giving elected figures a part in the government of the Empire, the new monarch came up against a no less difficult problem — drawing up a plan of policy for the state and putting it into effect with the aid of people he himself appointed. The position was complicated by the fact that the ministers the Emperor had inherited from his father did not hold a common view on the possible courses of Russia's development. To some extent their disagreements reflected the two-sided policy that prevailed in the last years of Alexander III's reign: efforts, on the one hand, to accelerate in every way possible the country's industrial and financial growth; on the other, to ensure for the future too a stable, conservative, agrarian Russia dominated by the nobility. This dichotomy expressed itself in a clash of sorts in the late nineteenth century between two powerful government bodies — the Ministry of Finance and the Ministry of Internal Affairs.

From Vladimir Gurko's book *The Tsar and Tsarina*:

Nicholas II forced himself to attend to the affairs of state, but essentially they did not captivate him. The enthusiasm for power was something alien to him. Ministers' reports were a heavy burden to him. The creative urge was lacking in him... The chief distinguishing feature of his character was an all-penetrating self-sacrificing devotion to the performance of what he considered his royal business...

Mild-natured and therefore incapable of forcing people to bow to the opinion that he expressed, he was, however, far from being weak-willed and on the contrary was marked by a stubborn striving to realise the intentions he formed... The main reason for the outward weak-will of Nicholas II that has been mentioned was his extreme natural delicacy that did not permit him to say anything unpleasant to anyone's face...

Nicholas viewed any taking of initiative on the part of his ministers as an attempt to usurp part of his own royal power... Given the absence in the sovereign's mind of a precise boundary between ruling and directing, in practice it turned out that the more business-like a particular minister was, the more he displayed activity and energy, the stronger the thought established itself in the Tsar's mind that this was an infringement of his, royal power and the sooner such a minister lost the royal trust. This was the very lot that befell Nicholas II's two most talented assistants — Witte and Stolypin...

While Nicholas II did not know how to command others, his own self-command was, by contrast, complete... If nothing else, we can judge Nicholas II's self-command by the fact that no-one saw him in raging anger or in joyful excitement, or even in a state of increased agitation... He took many matters very close to his heart, and some phenomena provoked him to very strong anger, which he nevertheless had the strength to hide completely behind a mask of calm and even indifference...

Exceptional self-possession gave the Tsar the strength to spend hours on end tirelessly reading the reports and detailed memoranda submitted to him. He saw this burdensome and for him uninteresting occupation as the main performance of his duty and did not shrink from it. "I shall never allow myself to go to bed," he said, "until I have completely cleared my desk."

Minister of Finance, Count Sergei Witte. St Petersburg. 1890s

Count Sergei Yulyevich Witte (1849–1915) is justly regarded as one of the greatest Russian statesmen at the turn of the twentieth century. As Minister of Finance between 1892 and 1903 Witte consistently pursued a policy of accelerated development for the nation's industry and consolidating the Russian budget. Among the highly important measures associated with his name were the introduction of an alcohol monopoly in 1895 and the gold rouble in 1897. Strong opposition in court circles and lack of support from Nicholas II obliged Witte to quit his post, but the upheavals of 1905 brought him back to the political stage. It was Witte who signed the peace treaty with Japan at Portsmouth, New Hampshire, acted as chief initiator of the Manifesto of 17 October, and first Chairman of the united Council of Ministers. After his resignation in April 1906, when the most critical moment of the revolution had already passed, Witte spent his remaining years in enforced idleness, although he continued to follow current affairs. The memorial to this period in his life are the three-volume *Memoirs* that give an extremely interesting picture of government and court circles in Russia in the late nineteenth and early twentieth centuries.

For all the contradictory nature of Witte's views his actions were founded on an entirely definite conception of the laws that characterised the development of the modern world. Speaking at one of the official meetings towards the end of the nineteenth century, he pointed out that a great historic revolution had already taken place in the majority of European countries — economic dominance had passed from the land-owning class to the class of industrialists and financiers.

In his opinion no country in the world could avoid such an upheaval within the next fifty years, still less Russia that had already embarked on that course. Proceeding from these views, Witte carried out a policy of encouraging in every way the faster industrial development of the country, supporting high customs barriers to protect the domestic market, a forced pace of railway construction, and state orders for the largest Russian enterprises. As it was exceptionally favourable to industrialists, a system of that kind caused appreciable damage to those making agricultural produce — first and foremost the owners of landed estates. From that developed the strong dislike for Witte in conservative noble circles who accused him of forgetting the interests of rural Russia so as to please international banks and stock exchange speculators. While protecting the economic interests of the growing Russian middle class, Witte was at that time far from any intention to make concessions to its political demands. Moreover, in his verbose memorandum *Autocracy and the Zemstvo*, the future chief initiator of the Manifesto of 17 October sought to show that the existing social order in Russia was organically incompatible with any sort of representation and an autocratic monarchy was the best expression of the national interests of the country. In the light of that, in the late nineteenth century he spoke out against the expansion of rural self-administration then being implemented. Like the majority of high state officials, Witte jealously guarded his bureaucratic power against any interference, even the most well-intentioned, still more against public control. For the aristocratic conservatives, however, Witte appeared to be a dangerous radical who was chipping away at the foundations of the Russian state.

Minister of Internal Affairs (1895–1899),Chairman of the Council of Ministers (1906, 1914–1916) Ivan Goremykin

NICHOLAS ROMANOV. Life and Death

Nicholas II's arrival on the throne did not change the new direction in the country's foreign policy that had finally taken shape in the last years of Alexander III's life. Although the late Emperor was followed to the grave almost immediately, in January 1895, by his long-time Minister of Foreign Affairs, Nikolai Girs, the young autocrat's adherence to his father's legacy in foreign affairs was never in doubt. The next few years provided plentiful confirmations of that.

The most important of these was the official acknowledgement of the existence of a political and military alliance between Russia and republican France, the establishment of which at the end of the last reign had been kept strictly secret. An overt affirmation of the alliance came in the shape of an official visit to Paris by the Russian Emperor in autumn 1896 and a return visit to St Petersburg by President Felix Faure. After that Europe became accustomed to Franco-Russian summit meetings, and the alliance of the two countries became a fixed quantity in the balance of great powers on the continent.

Equally traditional was the exchange of visits between the Russian and German monarchs, although the long-time allies had already managed to become rivals. There were still two decades left, though, to their direct clash on the battlefields of the First World War, and at the turn of the century Russo-German relations still preserved the semblance of warmth, something aided too by the good personal relationship between Tsar and Kaiser. Mutual understanding between the neighbouring powers was also strengthened by the agreement achieved in 1896−97 between two old rivals, Russia and Germany's closest ally Austria-Hungary, on the maintenance of peace in the Balkans for the next ten years. A symbol of the relative rapprochement was the appearance in St Petersburg of a rare guest for the northern capital — Emperor Franz Josef.

While there were no radical changes, there was a distinctive feature to foreign policy in the first years of Nicholas's reign: a noticeable increase in Russian attention to the East. In the second half of the 1890s there were increasingly frequent visits by senior figures from Asia — China, Japan and Siam.

Nicholas II (right) and King Victor Emmanuel III of Italy out hunting. Italy. 1900

In March 1898 Nicholas II spoke out in favour of international disarmament, a idea with which he was almost fifty years ahead of his time. A military man by upbringing and education, the Emperor was by his character a convinced opponent of war and arms-races.

The result of his noble initiative was the Hague Conference of 1899 at which Russian diplomats made and supported many proposals that were later incorporated into twentieth-century international law.

At that time the majority were not accepted by the remaining great powers who held to the dictum: "If you want peace, prepare for war."

Nevertheless something was achieved: it was decided, for example, to establish an international court of arbitration — a sort of prototype of the League of Nations and the UN Security Council.

A temporary piece of sculpture symbolising Franco-Russian friendship. It was set up in St Petersburg on the junction of Nevsky Prospekt and Mikhailovskaya Street for the visit of French President Emile Loubet. 1902. Photograph by K. Bulla

The Life-Guards Izmailovsky Regiment. Emperor Nicholas II and the regimental commander Major-General Kisilevsky inspecting the troops. Tsarskoye Selo. 17 May 1909

Although Russian foreign policy under Alexander III and Nicholas II was in general directed towards peace, the country's influence in European affairs remained founded to a large extent on the might of its armed forces. From its very appearance under Peter the Great, the Russian Empire acquired the image of a strongly militarised state, in which the army had become one of the most important institutions. It was no coincidence that many foreign, and indeed Russian (Alexander Herzen) observers compared Russia with imperial Rome. By the late nineteenth century the country possessed the largest army in the world — it numbered over 900,000 men, not counting the Cossack units. Military expenses amounted to some 300 million roubles a year, more than a fifth of the entire budget, and in this respect only neighbouring Germany could compete.

In the majority of Western states there was moreover a tendency to exaggerate the strength of the Russian army; it is not by chance that in French, German and British newspapers of the day you often come across assertions that "the Tsar holds the fate of peace in Europe in his hands."

Nicholas had a very serious regard for the Emperor's role as the commander-in-chief of the Russian armed forces.

The army was traditionally an object of special attention and concern for the reigning monarch, and scarcely a day went by when he did not receive someone from the military.

Inspections of the guards and the St Petersburg garrison, parades, attending military exercises, acquainting himself with new types of small arms and artillery, visits to forts and citadels under construction — between them these accounted for a considerable part of the Tsar's time. But even "off-duty", Nicholas had an liking for military men and all things military. According to many accounts, his favourite leisure activity was to visit gatherings of officers, mainly of the guards regiments, where he would hold simple, free and easy conversations with the line officers, kindred spirits, about the trivia of regimental life, appointments and promotions, hunting and horses. In this society Nicholas, by his own admission, "relaxed spiritually" and often sat up through the night.

Nicholas II receiving a report from the commander of H.M. Empress Maria Feodorovna's Life- and House-Guards Regiment, Prince Felix Yusupov, Count Sumarokov-Elston. Peterhof. 1904

Military uniform was the customary dress for other members of the House of Romanov too. Even the girls of the ruling dynasty were appointed patrons of guards regiments from birth, and from an early age took part in various reviews, parades and regimental festivities. As for the male sex, any grand duke was considered first and foremost an officer on active service; any other inclinations or pastimes were at best tolerated, but by definition less worthy activities.

Konstantin Konstantinovich had a poet's calling. In his diary he recorded the powerful feeling of annoyance and shame that his first verses evoked in his father, Konstantin Nikolayevich. The father reminded the son that Nicholas I "did not accept that a grand duke might even think of some activity beyond the service of the state." Alexander Mikhailovich also recollected the heavy silence with which relatives received his brother Georgy's childhood wish to become a portrait painter (the boy drew well). He also conveyed Nicholas II's opinion on the grand dukes' proper activities in life: "For three hundred years my fathers and grandfathers earmarked their relatives

for a military career. I do not want to break with that tradition."

The military capital of Russia was brilliant St Petersburg, glittering with the gold braid of elaborate uniforms. The guards units were located here, as well as the senior administrative bodies for the forces — the army and navy ministries, the General Staff and it celebrated Academy, the Chief Naval Staff, and a large number of military colleges and cadet corps. By the beginning of the twentieth century St Petersburg was probably the only capital in the world to have such a quantity of barracks and military installations in its central districts.

The Empire's military facade was magnificent, but in reality over the decades since Nicholas I much had changed and the role of the forces, the generals and the officer class in the life of the country had clearly declined. Yet the militarised aspects of court life and the glamorous parades of guards on the Field of Mars (which were abandoned after Alexander II and revived in the first year of Nicholas II's reign) were still regarded as enormously important.

NICHOLAS ROMANOV. Life and Death

The closing note of the winter military season in St Petersburg was the annual May parade on the Field of Mars. At the end of this "apotheosis of martial splendour", as the artist Alexander Benois wrote, recalling his childhood delight in the thousands upon thousands of "beloved soldiers", the guards regiments moved to their summer camp at Krasnoye Selo outside St Petersburg where the regimental training and cavalry muster took place. The main camp of tents intended for the infantry extended for some four miles along the slope down to the River Ligovka. The cavalry regiments installed themselves in the villages scattered around the training ground and there too were the officers' dachas, painted in the colours of their regiments. For a few weeks the whole character of the area was transformed. The roll of drums and soldiers' songs disrupted the customary quiet. Deafening salvoes rang out at the well-constructed shooting-ranges for all distances; cavalry squadrons turned, reformed and galloped across the hills. The culmination of these events were the large corps manoeuvres held in the presence of the sovereign that also effectively marked the end of the training period.

As General Ipatyev recollected "the Tsar's arrival turned the training camp for a few days into an unbroken society holiday." The famous Krasnoye Selo horse races still existed in just the same form as they are described in *Anna Karenina*. The Emperor presented prizes to the winners of the races in specially constructed pavilions, right by the stands. It was not just jockeys, however, who pitted their talents against each other, althought they were, of course, the "elite". During the camps genuine, and no less entertaining, "tournaments" were arranged between those skilled in the boiling of cabbage soup and porridge, for which purpose hollows were dug on the slopes of the uderhof Hills to take the kettles. The winners here were decided by the secret vote of a jury of sergeant majors.

The winners and the best marksmen also received their souvenir prizes from the Emperor's own hand.

After the races everybody took off in trokas, pairs or cabs to the Krasnoye Selo theatre, where the leading role in the ballet was played by Kschessinska, who was admired at once by all three of her successive most august lovers — Nicholas II himself, his young uncle Sergei Mikhailovich and the younger brother of the future pretender to the throne Kirill, the still very youthful Andrei.

On the following day all the company that had been in the theatre assembled shortly before sunset at the church of the main camp, where a "ceremonial retreat" was to take place.

A band drawn from all the guards regiments, about a thousand men, paraded in front of the grand tent, performing pieces of music that they had rehearsed earlier. In front of them, and a few paces from the Tsar stood the most senior drummer, the drummer of the Semenovsky Regiment, with a great grey beard. He waved his drumsticks and the music fell silent. The old man, turning smartly to the band, gave the command: "Hats off for prayer!", after which, in the last rays of the setting sun, he clearly and distinctly recited the Lord's Prayer.

Those attending the tattoo, the St Petersburg nobility, career staff officers and glittering guardsmen crowding around the ladies' stands regarded it as a necessary piece of ceremonial that had long-since lost its real meaning. The instant it was over they hastened off to the Krasnoye Selo theatre or to jolly dinners with showily-dressed ladies of all ranks who had come in from the capital.

The annual camp had finished and trains full to the point of overflowing took all the officer class back to the capital, while life in Krasnoye Selo went into suspension until the next spring...

Emperor Nicholas II and the high command taking a parade on the Field of Mars. St Petersburg. May 1903

General Ignatyev later had the opportunity to evaluate the true significance of all these army spectacles. When a few years later in the fields of Manchuria he was obliged to rack his brains over the causes of the catastrophic defeats suffered by the Russian army, in his mind's eye "there unfailingly appeared the picture of the May parade on the Field of Mars — that wicked mockery, that criminal self-deceit and sham, which had nothing in common with war... Sadly for the Russian army this divorcing of the troops' training from the real requirements of the art of warfare occurred not only on the Field of Mars, but also on the Training Ground of the camp at Krasnoye Selo. How many times in Manchuria did we former guardsmen say, when caught in some hard action: 'Yes, this isn't your Krasnoye Selo manoeuvres!'". Yet it was the St Petersburg military district and particularly, the great Krasnoye Selo camp that, another participant of those annual events, A.M. Zatonchkovsky, wrote, set "the tone for training throughout the Russian army". After the hard lessons of the Russo-Japanese War this became particularly noticeable: "Tremendous importance was acknowledged to lie in infantry, machine-gun and artillery fire, that was taken to the extreme (a regimental commander whose regiment failed to get excellent marks in the shooting review was supposed to submit his resignation) which unwittingly also led to certain undesirable peace-time tricks. An infantry advance was permitted only after real preparation with rifle, machine-gun and artillery fire."

The opening of the Krasnoye Selo camps. The officer of the day tries the food prepared in the field kitchen. Krasnoye Selo. 1907

Launch of the battleship *Pobeda* from the slipway of the Baltic Ship-Building and Mechanical Works. St Petersburg. 11 May 1900

In contrast to his father, Alexander III, Nicholas II liked to stress his interest in the navy and the country's maritime might. He frequently attended naval parades, the keel-laying or launching ceremonies for new fighting ships and invariably dressed in the uniform of a naval captain. Three of the grand dukes closest to the court — Alexei Alexandrovich, Alexander Mikhailovich and Kirill Vladimirovich — performed their military service in the navy, occupying various commanding positions in accordance with their ages.

Russia in the second half of the 1890s remained one of the greatest maritime powers, but its navy included many ships of outdated types and its main forces were concentrated, as they had been half a century before, on two land-locked seas — the Black Sea and the Baltic. More far-sighted people had long since warned of the dangers of such a position and pointed to the need to strengthen the country's naval positions in the Pacific and Arctic Oceans and to create new fighting squadrons of modern fast armourclads and cruisers.

At the end of the nineteenth century a large shipbuilding programme was initiated. A series of up to date fighting ships, corresponding to the changed demands of war at sea, were laid down in both Russian yards and some abroad. By the start of the Russo-Japanese War, however, that programme was still far from complete, while the majority of armourclads already built under it were lost in Port Arthur or at Tsushima.

After 1905 the Russian navy had to be recreated practically from scratch and in the years 1909—13 the construction of battleships — the type of armour-plated giants that had recently appeared — took place at a forced pace in the nations shipyards.

Emperor Nicholas II reviewing the crew of the battleship *Prince Suvorov* formed up on the quay of the Baltic Ship-Building and Mechanical Works. St Petersburg. 1902

The ice-breaker *Yermak*. 1899

NICHOLAS ROMANOV. Life and Death

St Petersburg's 200th anniversary was an event of great importance in the life of the capital. Preparation for it began well in advance. Jubilee almanacs and historical publications appeared. Exhibitions were held in different parts of the city: in the Yekaterinhof Palace — the first palace museum in St. Petersburg, which housed a collection of items that belonged to Peter the Great or were typical of his era; in the Summer Gardens; in Peter's Log Cabin, in the Technological Institute, where an extensive display related the rise in science in Peter's time and followed it up to the beginning of the twentieth century. The main festivities took place in the historic centre of the city: on St Isaac's and Peter I's (Decembrist) Squares, the Admiralty, Palace and Petrovsky Embankments, in the Peter and Paul Fortress and the Summer Gardens. Around the Bronze Horseman monument the coats-of-arms of the ruling House of Romanov were on display, a royal tent and places for guests of honour were set up. The whole city was a colourful display of flowers and flags, with which "the residents of the capital were permitted to decorate the houses on the day of 16th May..." One of main events during the celebrations was the ceremonial opening in the presence of members of the imperial family of the Trinity Bridge. This new crossing over the Neva was of immense importance to the city. Up until then the banks of the huge river had only been linked by two permanent bridges — the Nikolayevsky (now Lieutenant Shmidt) and Liteiny Bridges.

The rest were temporary pontoon bridges that could practically be used only in the summer and autumn months. On 16 May, the day of the main celebration to mark St Petersburg's jubilee, from early morning citizens filled the streets of the capital in their finest outfits — the appropriate form of attire had been laid down in advance: full dress uniform for those in the services; festive clothes for civilians. Palace Bridge and the old Trinity Bridge were drawn open. On the expanses of the Neva vessels of all classes stopped at anchor in a parade line of pre-planned order: the Guards Crew and Navy, the Imperial, St Petersburg River and other yacht clubs, early eighteenth-century galleys, other rowing vessels, steam launches and yachts.

The chief relic at the feast, the authentic symbol of Russian naval glory, was the small oak boat in which Peter the Great had learnt to sail. Delivered beforehand on a barge, it took part in the ceremonial procession, receiving all due honours as in Peter's time at the end of the Northern war.

On the instructions of the Most Holy Synod, services of thanksgiving were held in all the churches of the northern capital that day, after which the popular festivities began in the streets and squares.

The formal opening of Trinity Bridge. The head of the St Petersburg municipal administration Lelianov presents Emperor Nicholas II with a button connected to the raising mechanism. 16 May 1903

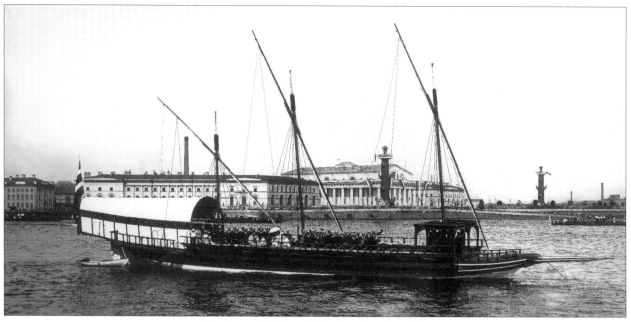

Members of the imperial family on board a yacht
on the day of St Petersburg's Bicentennial. 16 May 1903

Religious procession on Peter I Square on the day of St Petersburg's Bicentennial. 16 May 1903

The turn of the century proved a fateful boundary in the political history of the Empire. Discontent with the supreme ruler began to grow with especial pace after threatening signs appeared that the "period of calm" would soon end. Student disturbances as early as February 1899 indicated the growth of tension in the country, as a gravely alarmed Grand Duke Sergei Alexandrovich wrote to Nicholas from Moscow. The Emperor, by contrast, remained convinced of the enduring "calm of our boundless Russia" and saw the students' protest as nothing more than youthful over-excitement. The years immediately following showed, however, that "Uncle Sergei" was more perspicacious than his crowned nephew.

The new century opened with threatening events. The shot fired by the former student Karpovich at Nikolai Bogolepov, the Minister of Public Education, heralded the return of political terrorism that had seemed long-since defeated. In April of the following year the Social Revolutionary Balmashev killed Dmitry Sipiagin, the Minister of Internal Affairs, as the latter entered the State Council building in military uniform. In a letter to his mother, Dowager Empress Maria Fiodorovna, Nicholas wrote: "For me this is a very severe loss, because of all the ministers I trusted him the most, and also liked him as a friend. He performed his duty honestly and above-board. Everyone acknowledges that, even his enemies..." Society, however, was increasingly coloured by an attitude of liberal distaste for the authorities, all their undertakings and all their representatives, and Sipiagin's death was viewed almost as a feast of liberty. Among lawyers, professors, journalists, not to mention students, there were those who openly expressed sympathy with the minister's assassin. In the twenty years that had passed since the explosion on the Catherine Canal the public's views had had time to change radically and irreversibly.

Sipiagin's appointed successor, Viacheslav Plehve, proposed repressive measures to restore order in Russia. Tightening the police "screws", however, could not give the desired "calming effect" — that same year several southern provinces were affected by agrarian disturbances; the expression of opposition grew stronger in liberal, middle-class circles; and, most dangerously, the wave of political terror was rising ever higher. In only two years several provincial governors were slain, as were a large number of gendarme officers and particularly those who were regarded as "agent provocateurs" — the real or supposed police infiltrators into the revolutionary movement. Plehve himself fell victim to terrorism on 15 July 1904, when the Social Revolutionary Sazonov threw a bomb at his carriage. His funeral symbolised the collapse of the conservative course.

The deaths of people close to him, often those who shared his thinking, gravely affected the Emperor. Yet neither the outburst of terrorism, nor the increasingly frequent reports of rural unrest, industrial action, and growing murmurs among the educated populace could make Nicholas positively attempt to change the course of events in accordance with the demands of the time. As far as the Tsar was concerned he was the legitimate "master of the Russian land", exclusively answerable to God and to God alone for everything that took place in that land.

Viacheslav Plehve (1846–1904), Minister of Internal Affairs, head of the separate corps of gendarmes. St Petersburg. 1902

Events were, however, being less determined by the autocrat's will with every passing year. On top of the inexorably growing danger of revolution, there were serious complications in the Far East, that led ultimately to an ill-starred war with Japan.

On the whole Nicholas pursued a fairly cautious foreign policy. Back in 1896, for example, he had dismissed a suggestion made by the Russian ambassador in Constantinople and the head of the General Staff that Russia should exploit the domestic crisis in the Ottoman Empire and mount a surprise attack to gain possession of the fortified positions on the shore of the Bosphorus, and thus achieve a long-held geopolitical goal — to close the Black Sea to ships of hostile powers. Although Nicholas himself fully shared the feelings of those who called on him to "seize the moment", he did not risk such an active move for fear of provoking a Europe-wide conflict. In Russia's Far Eastern strategy, shaped to a large extent by the personal initiative of the Emperor, a due measure of statesmanly restraint was, however, lacking.

While for the greater part of the nineteenth century the attention of the Empire's military and diplomatic circles was riveted on the Balkans and the Black Sea straits, and in the 1870s and 1880s emphasis was placed on Russian expansion in Central Asia, towards the end of the century the eyes of the St Petersburg ruling clique turned ever more often to the shores of the Pacific. The political preference for the Far East was founded on the erroneous conception that the area contained no powerful opponents or rivals for Russia. China was in deep decline. The British spheres of influence lay much further south. There were few Russian statesmen in that period who took Japan seriously. As far back as 1880, Admiral-General Grand Duke Konstantin Nikolayevich had written in his report for Alexander II's silver jubilee that "the time is approaching when not the Baltic or Black Sea ports, but ports on the Great Eastern Ocean will become the harbours of a new Russian fleet." To that end, as early as 1898, Russia leased the Laiodong Peninsula with the right to establish a naval base at Port Arthur from a China weakened by its recent defeat in the war with Japan. After the tremendous popular uprising of 1900–01 in China that was suppressed by the intervention of the great powers (the Russian forces in Manchuria were actively involved, entering Peking under the command of General Linevich), Russia's expansionist plans in the Far East developed still further. Attempts to implements them, however, met with ever-increasing resistance from Japan, a new great power that became the chief opponent of Russian influence in Manchuria and Korea.

In Russian ruling circles there were various opinions on how best to achieve the country's strategic aims in the Far East. The most aggressive stance was taken by the "party of force" among whom were Admiral Alexeyev, the governor-general of the Far East, a number of figures close to the court, including, it was claimed, Grand Duke Alexander Mikhailovich, and several leading people in the War Ministry. A more cautious attitude was taken by Vladimir Lamsdorf, the Foreign Minister, and Sergei Witte, the Finance Minister; they proposed economic absorption of Manchuria rather than military-administrative measures and warned against a worsening of relations with Japan.

Nicholas himself most probably sympathised with the "party of force", but he was clearly not seeking a war, believing that little Japan "would not dare" to make the first move against the Russian giant. In the long drawn-out negotiations with the island empire Russia made concessions, but an aggressively-minded Tokyo demanded much more. In the circumstances Nicholas and those around him seriously underestimated Japan's military might and its resolve to use force in its dispute with Russia.

On 26 January 1904 news came from the Far East of a surprise attack by the Empire of the Rising Sun. The raid by Japanese torpedo-boats on Russian ships lying at anchor off Port Arthur preceded the declaration of war.

NICHOLAS ROMANOV. Life and Death

Alexei Kuropatkin, who was appointed commander-in-chief of the army in the Far East was, in the opinion of those who knew him well, a fine military administrator and staff officer, but lacked any great gifts as a commander in the field. Nevertheless the strategy he adopted was probably the most correct in the circumstances — considering the remoteness and small population of the Far East, he reckoned it sensible to avoid major battles with the enemy troops that were continuously being reinforced from their nearby homeland. Gradually wearing them down in small defensive actions, the Russian army was to withdraw into the depths of what was by the standards of the day an immense theatre of war, thus stretching the enemy's lines of communication and luring him away from the sea where the Japanese navy was dominant. But Kuropatkin found his hands tied by those who demanded rapid, impressive victories and the relief of the beleaguered base at Port Arthur. As a result of such pressure, the commander was obliged, against his better judgement, to risk major clashes — and more often than not they ended in failure.

The Emperor's thoughts and feelings were all with his army in the field, but the character of the war taking place in distant Manchuria did not give him the opportunity to take personal charge of military operations. Nicholas was forced to spend most of his time travelling around European Russia, inspecting troops bound for the East and attending church services where God was asked to send Russia victory. Yet there was no real upsurge of patriotic feeling in the country.

In the morning the grave and inexpressibly sad news came", Nicholas II wrote on 31 March, *"that while our squadron was returning to Port Arthur, the battleship Petropavlovsk struck a mine, was blown up and sank with the loss of Adm. Makarov, most of the officers and crew. Kirill, slightly injured, Yakovlev — the captain, a few officers and sailors — all wounded — were rescued. The whole day I could not get this terrible misfortune out of my mind...*

Nicholas II visits troops departing for the front during the Russo-Japanese War. Poltava, Ukraine. 1904

War Minister Alexei Kuropatkin (1848–1925) in the office of the ministry. February 1904

The military failures led to an even greater decline in the prestige of the Emperor and of the army high command who were traditionally close to him. From autumn 1904 opposition actions became ever bolder in character, and the situation was further complicated by a rapid growth in national separatist sentiment on the fringes of the Empire. All this became particularly obvious after the fall, in December 1904, of Russia's Far Eastern stronghold — the fortress of Port Arthur, the defence of which had become a sort of symbol of Russian determination in the war. The report of the capitulation came on 21 December, as the Emperor was on the imperial train in Byelorussia. "Received staggering news from Stessel in the night," Nicholas wrote as neatly as ever, "about the surrender of Port Arthur to the Japanese in the light of immense losses and disease among the garrison, and the complete lack of shells! It's hard and painful, although it had been foreseen, but one wanted to believe that the army would come to the aid of the fortress. The defenders are all heroes and did more than could have been expected. It was God's will then!"

The fall of Port Arthur became a prologue to the first Russian revolution.

Emperor Nicholas II with an icon of Christ the Saviour giving parting encouragement to the 148th Caspian regiment of Foot before its departure for the front in Manchuria. Peterhof. 1905. Photograph by K. Bulla

The Time of Difficult Decisions

The year 1905 was a milestone of change in both Russian history and the life of Emperor Nicholas II and his family. The beginning of the year was tragically marred by the events of 9 January in St Petersburg — the "Bloody Sunday" that shook the monarchy to its very foundation, unleashing the destructive forces of national revolution. At its end came another event, little noted at the time, but no less fatal in the long run for the dynasty and the empire — the "man of God" Grigory Rasputin first came into contact with the imperial family.

The Emperor — living in constant fear over the health of his son, and weighed down by the depressing news from the theatre of the Russo-Japanese War (in February the Battle of Mukden was lost; in May Russia was stunned by Tsushima which demolished the country's naval might) — received daily reports of outbursts of revolutionary violence, a tremendous wave of strikes, armed uprisings with fighting on the barricades, and mutinous army units. A certain share of the responsibility for this sinister chronicle lay directly with Nicholas — the beginning had come with the shooting down of thousands of St Petersburg workers who on that January Sunday sought to present a peaceful petition at the Winter Palace.

Much still remains unclear about the events leading up to the tragedy of Bloody Sunday — first and foremost, perhaps, the degree of actual danger that might have been presented by an enormous procession of people, up to 140,000 strong. The measures taken by the authorities in advance of 9 January were, however, more like preparations to repulse an enemy army from the administrative districts of the capital than ordinary efforts to maintain law and order. The troops who blocked the streets leading to the centre of St Petersburg had orders to open fire if the demonstrators continued their march despite a ban. Whether a tragic misunderstanding or a deliberate provocation, the actions to stop the workers' demonstrations at the Narva Gate, on the Petersburg Side, and on Palace Square itself turned into a bloody massacre. By some reckonings more than 1,200 people died on that day and about 5,000 more were injured. Among the victims were women and children.

The tragedy of Bloody Sunday roused the country and became the detonator for the first Russian revolutionary explosion. As the pro-monarchist historian S.S. Oldenburg wrote: "on 9 January ... it emerged that not only the intelligentsia, but also the 'common people' — at least in the cities — were to a considerable extent in the ranks of the opponents of the existing order." Workers' strikes gripped the industrial centres: in January 1905 alone the number of strikers amounted to over 440,000 — more than in the whole of the preceding decade. The influence of extreme left-wing parties calling for an open armed struggle with those in power increased sharply. With the spring a rapid rise of the peasant movement began, frequently spilling over into the robbery and burning of estate manor houses, the murder of representatives of the authorities, and the spontaneous seizure and redistribution of land.

"The police on the spot were in panic. From all the provinces there arose cries for help and requests to send guards units or Cossacks. So many governors were killed that an appointment to that post was tantamount to a death sentence," a contemporary remembered. Anti-governmental, and in many instances overtly separatist actions seized the non-Russian fringes of the Empire, most notably Finland, the Kingdom of Poland, the Baltic lands and the Caucasian provinces. Particularly threatening for the future of the monarchy was the rapid growth of mutinous thinking in the forces, which became obvious after the uprising on the battleship *Potemkin* in June 1905 that echoed like thunder across the whole of Russia.

The opening of the Kolomna section of the Assembly of Russian Factory Workers. In the centre is that man who would organise the popular procession to the Winter Palace, the priest Georgy Gapon, together with the city administrator I.A. Fullon. November 1904. Photograph by K. Bulla

"*Every child's hat, mitten, or woman's headscarf lying pitifully abandoned on the St Petersburg snow that day remained a reminder that the Tsar should die, that the Tsar will die...*" Osip Mandelstam remembered. Gorky's response to these events was the furious article Bloody Sunday in which he recreated the dreadful scenes on Palace Square: "*People dropped in twos and threes, crouching on the ground, clutching their stomachs, running somewhere, limping, clambering throught the snow, and all across the snow a mass of bright red spots broke out. They spread, steaming, catching the eye. The crowd fell back, stopped for a moment, frozen, and suddenly a wild, startling howl rang out from hundreds of throats.*" Another witness to the tragedy, Valentin Serov, wrote to his fellow artist Ilya Repin: "*What I was obliged to witness from the Academy of Arts on 9 January is something I shall never forget — a well-behaved, dignified unarmed crowd walking into cavalry charges and the sights of rifles — a terrible spectacle. What I heard later was still more incredibly horrific. Can it really be that the Tsar's not wishing to come out to the workers and receive their request meant that they were to be massacred? Who decided that this massacre was to occur? Nobody and nothing can wipe out this stain.*"

Meeting by the building of St Petersburg University. 18 October 1905

NICHOLAS ROMANOV. Life and Death

In a situation where revolution had spread across the country, autocratic power was left effectively in complete isolation. Demands for the implementation of "popular representation" could be heard everywhere in that period — at the political banquets of the liberal intelligentsia and in the revolutionary strike committees of the mines and factories. Even such newspapers as *Sankt-Peterburgskiye Vedemosti*, *Svet* and *Novoye Vremya* until recently loyal to the government, even the conservative Russian Assembly and one of its ideologists, the courtier General Kireyev, advocated the summoning of a *zemsky sobor* — a kind of general assembly last seen in the seventeenth century — as "a national form of representation". In the new circumstances resisting claims that were by now almost universal became ever harder. Two weeks after the death of Grand Duke Sergei Alexandrovich, one of the most implacable advocates of firm autocracy, killed in Moscow on 4 February by the Socialist Revolutionary Kaliayev, the Emperor began to make concessions.

On 19 February the government published instructions, signed by Nicholas the day before, to the new Minister of the Interior Bulygin, that referred to the intention "to involve the men most worthy of the people's trust, empowered and elected by the population in the preliminary drafting and discussion of legislative proposals." The idea was to establish an elected consultative chamber, whose rights and powers would be similar to the functions of the State Council of years past.

The plan for the State Duma drawn up under Bulygin's direction by July 1905 was examined at the meetings that took place at Peterhof between 18 and 26 July with the Emperor himself chairing. Involved in the discussions were the grand dukes, ministers, prominent members of the State Council and senators, as well as the outstanding historian Professor Vasily Kliuchevksy. But the draft law approved at that time and published on 6 August failed to satisfy almost everybody: in the incandescent atmosphere of revolutionary disturbances the proposal to create a consultative Duma looked like a document from the historical archives, a relic of the remote past.

The political crisis in the country continued to deepen: in October Russia was seized by another wave of strikes that advanced two main demands — an eight-hour working day and the summoning of a constituent assembly. The stoppages on the railways that began on 15 October developed into a general strike involving over two million people in almost all branches of industry. The situation was becoming ever more threatening.

As many close to the Emperor later testified in that October he was faced with a difficult choice between two possible courses of action. The first consisted, in the words of Prince Obolensky, in "granting unlimited dictatorial powers to some trusted person so as to suppress energetically and irrevocably at the root any hint of the appearance of any resistance to the government, albeit at the expense of mass bloodshed." Such an approach was psychologically acceptable to Nicholas and the majority of the men around him. They must, however, have been aware of the extreme danger of such a decision — direct military suppression of the revolution required the unswerving reliability of the army, and the former conviction that that was the case had been lost. It is no coincidence that not one of the "strongmen" in the Emperor's milieu — neither his close associate General Dmitry Trepov, appointed Governor-General of St Petersburg in 1905, nor Grand Duke Nikolai Nikolayevich — accepted the role of military dictator in a campaign against the revolution. The latter even threatened to "put a bullet through his head" according to the account of Vladimir Fredericks, the Minister of the Imperial Court, who called on him to lead a dictatorship.

Failing that, it was necessary to "go over to making concessions to public opinion and to outline for the future cabinet instructions to embark on a constitutional course." This was the variant insisted upon by Witte who had recently returned from representing Russia at the peace talks with Japan held in the USA. The Treaty of Portsmouth signed on 21 August was relatively favourable for the defeated Empire — territorial losses in the Far East were slight and the inevitable blow to the prestige of the state less than might have been expected. For his services Witte was made a count and during the October crisis he proved probably the only political figure in the ruling camp with a far-reaching plan of action.

In the report presented to the Emperor on 9 October, Witte tried to demonstrate that the state

A treasury vehicle with a dead horse on the embankment of the Catherine canal following an attack by Socialist Revolutionaries who took valuables to the amount of 398,772 roubles and 24 kopecks. St Petersburg. 14 October 1906

authorities should again, as in the time of Alexander II, take the initiative of transformations into their own hands. "The goal has been set by society; its significance is great and wholly invincible, because there is truth in that goal. The government should therefore adopt it. The slogan "Freedom" should become the slogan of government actions. There is no other way in which the state can be saved... The course of historical progress is unstoppable... There is no choice: either assume the leadership of the movement that has gripped the country or abandon it to be torn apart by elemental forces. Executions and rivers of blood will only hasten the explosion."

The next few days in autumnal Peterhof passed in endless discussion. The Emperor felt a profound distrust of both Witte personally and his programme, sticking to the convictions that he had expressed in December 1904, on the eve of the revolutionary disturbances: "The peasant won't understand a constitution, but he'll understand only one thing: that the Tsar's hands have been tied, and then — my congratulations, gentlemen!" Yet it was not only Witte or his fellow-thinker Prince Obolensky, who produced the draft manifesto "on improving the state system", but also that long-time opponent of the former Minister of Finance Ivan Goremykin, who also discussed the issue with the Emperor, and Grand Duke Nikolai Nikolaye-vich, and even his foreign friend Kaiser Wilhelm II, who ten years before had hailed the young autocrat's "excellent speech" on the "impossible dreams" of the Tver *zemstvo* — everyone around was calling on him to give way, predicting an inevitable catastrophe otherwise. Having submitted to the general pressure the Emperor wrote to General Trepov on 16 October: "Yes, Russia is being granted a constitution. We were few in number who fought against it. But support was not forthcoming from any quarter in this struggle, every day an even greater number of people turned away from us and in the end the inevitable happened... Nevertheless, following my conscience I prefer to grant everything at once than to be obliged in the near future to make concessions on minor matters and arrive at the same point anyway." Vladimir Gurko wrote later of Nicholas that "throughout the whole of his reign he only once took an important decision in defiance of his inner desires, under pressure from one of his ministers, and that was on 17 October 1905 with the establishment of representation of the people."

NICHOLAS ROMANOV. Life and Death

The events surrounding the drafting and signing of the
Manifesto of 17 October brought the figure of Sergei Witte
back to centre stage. From a dignitary in disfavour not long
before, he turned into the key political figure of those months,
who was expected to take decisive, effective measures to
restore order and calm in a country convulsed by revolution,
but on a new basis — the basis of the rule of law and collabo-
ration with society. The first step along that road was to be
the creation of a united government, something Russia had
not had until then. Every minister was entirely independent
from his colleagues, appointed directly by the Emperor and
answerable only to him; regular co-ordination between the
work of different bodies was completely non-existent.
The same day that the Manifesto of 17 October appeared, it
was announced that the Emperor had "entrusted Count Witte
with unifying the activities of the ministers." This meant that
for the first time in Russia he was asked to form a single
cabinet and the newly-appointed Chairman of the Council of
Ministers arose before the country in a cloud of stately glory.
The new government was made up mainly of people from
Witte's circle, although an exception was made regarding the
four most important portfolios: the Ministries of War, the
Navy, Foreign Affairs and the Imperial Court were left as
before to the personal choices of the autocrat. Nevertheless,
a united government was created and represented a serious
transformation in the way the Russian state was organised.
This cabinet proved short-lived, however. The arm uprising in
Moscow in December 1905, anarchy on the country's railways,
the growth of agrarian terror against estate-owners and
wealthy bosses rapidly demolished the at one point almost
universal impression of Count Witte as a highly capable,
indeed irreplaceable statesman. His influence began to decline
rapidly and when, on 13 April 1906, he was obliged to tender
his resignation, Nicholas II accepted it with a feeling of
immense relief. In his eyes Witte was the man chiefly responsible for 17 October which had led to his autocracy losing its
previous total, unrestricted nature. The deep and mutual
dislike between the Emperor and his first premier lasted until
the final days of Witte's life.

Count Sergei Witte. St Petersburg. 1905

Piotr Nikolayevich Durnovo (1845–1915),
a lawyer by education, began his career as public prosecutor in
the town of Rybinsk on the Volga. Between 1884 and 1893 he
was head of the Department of Police, then a senator, Assistant
Minister of Internal Affairs, and director-general of the post and
telegraph service. From October 1905 he was Minister of
Internal Affairs and later State Secretary in the State Council
where he was one of the leaders of the right wing.

Minister of Internal Affairs, Piotr Durnovo. St Petersburg. 1906

**Nicholas II reading the manifesto on the opening of the First State Duma in St George's Room of the Imperial Winter Palace.
St Petersburg. 27 April 1906. Photograph by K.Ye. von Gan**

The Manifesto of 17 October marked an extremely important turning-point in the political history of Russia. While legally remaining an autocratic monarch, Nicholas in actual fact lost his former unlimited power and, most importantly, his unaccountability.. Elections to a State Duma meant the creation of popular representation in Russia. Although the first attempts at "parliamentarism" proved unsuccessfully — both the First and Second Dumas were dissolved in quick succession because of the dominance of the opposition parties that had formed in the few brief months of the revolution, the Russian Empire from that moment turned irrevocably into a representative monarchy.

A session of the First State Duma in the building of the Noble Assembly. St Petersburg. April 1906

The events of 1905 and 1906 signified a radical change in the structure of the Russian Empire as a state: it effectively ceased to be an autocratic monarchy, for all that it remained that in name. The new version of *The Basic Laws of the State* published on 23 April 1906 established that from that time on the Emperor wielded legislative power in unison with the State Council and the Duma — effectively a two-chamber parliament. All the male population was allowed to participate, but the voting was indirect, through electoral colleges — of landowners, municipalities, peasants and workers — who elected delegates to provincial assemblies and only from there were the over-whelming majority of deputies elected to the Duma. Such a system led to an enormous imbalance of voting-power at the elections — provincial Russia was given a considerable advantage over the industrial centres, and landowners over all other categories of elector. Despite the artificially created majority of conservative forces in the Duma, it still failed to become an entirely obedient tool in the hands of the govern-ment. Even the overtly right-wing parties were not always prepared to collaborate with the ruling bureaucracy, and ringing denouncements of "the irresponsibility of certain spheres" and "the court clique" were made, probably, by all the camps. Not trusting the Duma's loyalty, the government created a sort of counterweight in the form of the State Council. According to the decree of 20 February 1906, a portion of its members were elected by a complex system based on estates and corporations, while the rest were appointed directly by the Emperor. This led to the State Council consisting mainly of retired senior officials and men who enjoyed the trust of the court. Towards the end of Stolypin's life, when he had lost the support of right-wing circles, it was the State Council that ever more frequently hindered the continuation of his reforming activities.

The legislative rights of the two chambers were equal, which in practice meant that the State Council could block any resolution made by the Duma.

The Russian Empire turned after the reforms of 1906 not into a parliamentary monarchy but into a representational monarchy. The chief distinguishing feature of that kind of state structure, found in contemporary Germany and Austria-Hungary as well, was that the government was responsible only to the monarch, and not to the legislature. It was for precisely that reason that the basic demand of the legal opposition in the period leading up to the First World War and later — following the defeats of 1915 — was for a "responsible government". Nicholas, however, right up to his final days in power was unswerving in his rejection of a parliamentary cabinet, considering it fatal for the future of Russia. Only on the eve of the abdication, when everything was already lost, did he give his consent to the formation of a government answerable to the Duma — but it was already too late, the monarchy was doomed...

Piotr Arkadyevich Stolypin (1862–1911)

justly deserves recognition as the last major reformer in the history of the Russian Empire. The offspring of an old noble family, he proved himself a strong, capable administrator in several gubernatorial posts. In April 1906 he was appointed Minister of Internal Affairs, and in July Chairman of the Council of Ministers. Through energetic and at times savage measures he succeeded in restoring order to a country seized by revolts and disturbances. Perhaps the reason for Stolypin's passionate uncompromising attitude to revolutionary anarchy lay in part in a shock to him personally: on 12 August 1906 terrorists blew up his dacha on one of the St Petersburg islands. Thirty-two people were killed, including the bombers themselves, while the injured included the fourteen-year-old daughter and three-year-old son of the head of government. Stolypin himself was not hurt, but given his deep attachment to his family, this became a private reason to fight against the revolutionaries. Stolypin understood that internal calm in the country was necessary not only for its own sake, but also as a precondition for the successful realisation of his extensive programme of transformations. The agrarian reform initiated by the decree of 9 November 1906 was to be only the first step in the creation of a "great Russia" to which Stolypin directed all his efforts. However, the scope and far-sightedness of his thinking as a statesman were not always appreciated by those around him. The reformer's gradually growing isolation in ruling circles together with the lack of interest and support on the part of the Emperor were grounds for Stolypin to reflect bitterly on his lot during the last months of his life. Many believed that his political career was drawing to a close. The shot fired in Kiev in September 1911 only underlines the tragic fate of this gifted and determined man who might have represented Russia's last chance to avoid the "great shocks" to come.

The government's struggle against the revolution soon became a harsh one. In reply to armed uprisings in the cities, mutinies in the army and navy, the mass sacking of landed estates across the country and the incessant revolutionary terror — in 1906 alone 768 representatives of the authorities were killed and 820 injured — ever more extensive use was made of courts martial and banishment without trial to remote provinces. In the years 1907–09 more than 3,500 people were executed for "subversive activities"; tens of thousands were banished. The noted publicist Vladimir Korolenko wrote at that time of death sentences as "an everyday occurrence".
The Constitutional Democrat Fiodor Radichev referred to the noose in the Duma chamber as "a Stolypin necktie". Responding to his critics, while the debates about courts martial were still going on in the Second Duma, Stolypin said that Russia was "able to distinguish between the blood on the hands of executioners and the blood on the hand of honest doctors who took perhaps the most extraordinary measures, but with one hope, one wish — to cure a seriously ill patient!" The Emperor shared his opinion:
"The court martial operates... Let it operate with all the rigour of the law. There is not and cannot be another means of struggling with people who have become brutalised." The brutality grew on both sides of the barricades.

Piotr Stolypin, Minister of the Internal Affairs, Chairman of the Council of Ministers. St Petersburg. 1907

The Third Duma, formed in 1907 on the basis of a new electoral law, became a reliable partner for the government headed by a new "strongman", Piotr Stolypin, who advanced a wide-ranging programme of reforms vital to the country. His famous statement that for regeneration all Russia needed was "twenty years of peace at home and abroad" is evidence of his grasp of the immense potential for step-by-step reform in the country.

Nicholas undoubtedly respected Stolypin as a man who by firm, energetic measures had managed to restore order to an Empire gripped by revolution. He also acknowledged his genuine understanding of the sore points of Russian reality and supported his activities aimed at resolving them in the quickest possible time. Without the aid of the Emperor, Stolypin would never have managed to carry out his key reforms that met with quite strong opposition in the upper echelons of Russian bureaucracy. Yet it is equally clear that Nicholas mentally resisted the over-insistent guidance of his premier whose powerful personality often overshadowed the figure of the head of state in this period. The majority of the Emperor's immediate circle was also set against Stolypin.

NICHOLAS ROMANOV. Life and Death

As time went by, his influence declined appreciably and in the months before the tragic death of this last outstanding reformer in Tsarist Russia the inevitability of his early dismissal was widely mooted. On 1 September 1911, however, during the celebrations in Kiev to mark the unveiling of a monument to Alexander II, an event attended by the Emperor and senior officials, Stolypin was fatally wounded at the theatre by the police informer Bogrov.

The full story behind this murder has still not been established. At one time there were suggestions that the "court clique" was involved. It is hard to say whether that was really the case, but the fact that Nicholas chose not to attend Stolypin's funeral was seen by many as a sign of indifference towards his premier. The course of state policy did not, incidentally, change — the new chairman of the Council of Ministers was Vladimir Kokovtsov, a close associate of Stolypin, although lacking his predecessor's authority and energetic determination.

There was a certain foundation to the rumours going around the country about "shadowy influences" at court hostile to Stolypin. It was at just this time that the appearance of Grigory Rasputin close to the throne became fairly general knowledge and the most fantastic tales were circulating about his relationship with the imperial family. It was known that Stolypin had attempted to put an end to this, rightly believing that such a figure would inflict irreparable damage on the prestige of the ruling dynasty. In the spring of 1911 he had had a long talk with the Emperor, providing him with documentary evidence that blackened the image of the "man of God".

Nicholas's response is curious, indicating just how much he found himself a hostage to fate in this burning question: "I know and believe, Piotr Arkadyevich, that you are sincerely devoted to me. Perhaps everything you are telling me is the truth, but I ask you never to speak to me again about Rasputin. There is nothing that I can do anyway."

The imperial couple were introduced to Rasputin exactly two weeks after the signing of the Manifesto of 17 October — at a hard, troubled time for Nicholas and his wife. The Emperor first mentioned him in his diary on 1 November 1905:

"We drank tea with Militsa and Stana. Met a man of God — Grigory from Tobolsk province." It was then Grand Duchesses Militsa and Anastasia, the wives of Piotr and Nicholas Nikolayevich, who introduced the Siberian *starets* to the imperial family. Such encounters and spiritual discussions with people marked out by divine grace were a common occurrence at court in this period. In contrast to many, many others, however, Rasputin managed to establish himself in a completely unique position with respect to the first family of Russia.

Nicholas and Alexandra lived in constant fear for their son, little Alexis, whose illness left practically no room for hope and they were prepared to believe and to open their hearts to anyone who might save him from the incessant danger. That was just what Rasputin became, as he undoubtedly possessed supernatural powers the nature of which is still a scientific mystery today.

Rasputin's very appearance was striking and practically everyone who recalled him mentioned his extraordinary individuality and immense inner power which radiated from his stare.

From Maurice Paléologue's diary for 24 February 1915:
A tall man, dressed in a long black caftan of the kind wealthy peasants wear on feast days, with rough boots on his feet. Long, black, badly combed hair; a thick black beard; high forehead; a broad bulbous nose, muscular mouth. But all the expression of his face is concentrated in the cornflower-blue eyes, glinting, deep, strangely attractive. His look is at one and the same time penetrating and gentle, naive and cunning, intent and distant. When his speech grows animated, his pupils seem to become charged with magnetism.

From the memoirs of Vladimir Bonch-Bruyevich:
My attention was caught above all by his eyes: an intense and direct look, some phosphorescent light seemed to play in his audience with his eyes, and sometimes his speech suddenly slowed, he drew out the words, lost his track as if he were thinking of something else and stared fixedly at someone, steadily, right into their eyes, and stayed like that for some minutes, all the time slurring his words in an almost unintelligible manner. I noticed that it was that fixed stare in particular which had an effect on those present, especially the women.

Grigory Rasputin (Novykh) with Major-General M.S. Putiatin, a Special Envoy for the Administration of the Marshal of the Court (right) and D.N. Loman, Colonel of the Life-Guards Pavlovsky Regiment. St Petersbrug. 1904–05

NICHOLAS ROMANOV. Life and Death

The phenomenon of Rasputin, a simple Siberian peasant of wild, indomitable character and inexhaustible vital energy, who by some unknown means managed to carve out a dizzying career for himself, still remains in many ways a conundrum. There are many gaps and grey areas in his biography. A horse-thief in his youth and a debauchee noted for his taste for wild excesses, beaten and hauled before the courts on several occasions on charges of stealing poles, he belonged wholly to that category of possessed people of whom Dostoyevsky wrote, "you never know ahead of time whether they will enter a monastery or set fire to the village." At some point in the Verhoturye Monastery, where Rasputin had fled to escape the rage of his fellow-villagers, he underwent a spiritual transformation. He gave up his former way of life, stopped drinking, smoking and eating meat, and learnt to read Church Slavonic. It was then that his travels around the holy sites of Russia began. He visited dozens of monasteries and even made a pilgrimage to Jerusalem about which he subsequently composed brief *Meditations* Through his natural intelligence, as well as numerous meetings and talks with both members of the regular clergy and various sect members, wanderers and holy fools, Rasputin, by numerous accounts, had a good command of Scripture and was capable of interpreting it in his own independent fashion. He was also quite often seen in a state of prayer-induced ecstasy. This was evidently one more manifestation of an unrestrained nature that was confirmed again and again in the material of the Extraordinary Investigative Commission of the Provisional Government that examined Rasputin's case: "Some of them say that Rasputin could dance for hours on end. Others, Filippov, for example, relate that in the last period of his life, the period of madness and orgies, Rasputin could drink and make merry from 12 noon to 4 a.m., then go off to matins, stand through the service until 8 a.m. and then, after going home and drinking tea, until 2 p.m. receive as if nothing had happened the petitioners [who came to him in droves practically every day]."

Apart from his powerful energy, Rasputin undoubtedly possessed a hypnotic gift and a truly unique talent for healing, which was essentially what determined his meteoric rise. While he was uneducated, he had a fairly extensive knowledge of folk remedies and made confident use of the medicinal properties of Siberian, Tibetan and Chinese herbs. Yet what he achieved without the use of any supplementary means bordered on the miraculous. "If anyone had a bad head and was feverish", his personal secretary Simanovich, for example, recalled, "Rasputin stood behind the patient, took his head in his hands, whispered something no one could understand, and pushed the patient with the words 'Be off!' The patient felt he had got better. I experienced the effect of Rasputin's incantation myself and must acknowledge that it was staggering." Literally one session with Rasputin was enough to put Simanovich's own son, considered incurably ill, back on his feet.

According to some sources, from late 1907 onwards Rasputin's intervention, in the form of "holy prayer" for Tsesarevich Alexis saved the boy's life on several occasions. Perhaps his many skills did include the ability to affect the behaviour of the blood, something beyond the power of the best medicine of the day.

From General Vladimir Gurko's book *The Tsar and Tsarina*:

As the circle of people who indulged Rasputin grew, as he himself accumulated funds, his passionate, carnal nature increasingly gained the upper hand, while the divine inspiration, and even religiousness disappeared little by little. Wild drinking bouts, occasionally accompanied by scandals, occurred with increasing frequency and acquired an almost chronic character... Increased consumption of wine, a passionate inclination for and shameless pursuit of women emerged ever more clearly and became known among ever-broadening circles... As rumours of Rasputin's influence spread, and his influence had indeed grown considerably, various cunning people resolved to exploit it to achieve their own ends using him as the means... This all led to Rasputin arranging formal consultation hours and the number of those who came to them reached many dozens. Among the people who approached him for help of one kind or another, alongside those who backed up their request with material offerings or the promise of large sums, were also those who brought nothing and even themselves requested financial assistance. Strange as it may seem at first sight, Rasputin tried to help both the one group and the other... To play a prominent role, to be respected for his omnipotence, to become the equal of people whose social status placed them immeasurably above him — all that flattered his vanity and he willingly supported even those requests, fulfilment of which brought him personally no direct advantages.

Rasputin's gift revealed itself most strikingly in the autumn of 1912 when the Tsesarevich nearly died as the consequence of a minor knock that occurred while the family were at the hunting grounds in Poland. The internal bleeding that followed resulted in the formation of an enormous haematoma. The doctor's admitted that the boy's condition was extremely serious. Rasputin was not at hand, but a telegram he sent saved the situation — the mysterious force could operate at a distance. Citing this incident in his book *With the Tsar and Without the Tsar*, the palace commandant General Voyeikov wrote: "If one adopts the viewpoint of the Empress and mother, who regarded Rasputin as a god-fearing *starets*, whose prayers had helped her sick son, much should be understood and pardoned... The aid provided to the heir strengthened Rasputin's position at court so much that he no longer needed the support of the grand duchesses and members of the clergy."

The faith Nicholas and Alexandra Fiodorovna had in Rasputin grew even further when, some two years later, he saved from apparently certain death the Empress's intimate friend Anna Vyrubova, after a railway accident had left her with shattered legs, concussion and a fractured skull. This incident on 2 January 1915 made a powerful impression on those who witnessed it and became widely known. "When she was pulled out of the wreckage", Prince Andronnikov said, retelling under examination the story as he heard it from Yelizaveta Naryshkina, lady-in-waiting, head of the Empress's household, and, by the way, no friend of Rasputin, "the poor woman kept shouting 'Father, father, help me' (meaning Rasputin). She believed that he would help her... And that's what did happen... He dashed off to Tsarskoye Selo. When he arrived at Tsarskoye, the injured Vyrubova was surrounded by the former Tsar, the Tsarina, the whole royal family, the daughters I mean, and several doctors. Vyrubova was in a completely hopeless state. When Rasputin arrived, he bowed, came up to her and began making some kind of gestures and saying 'Annushka, can you hear me?' And she, after not saying anything to anyone, suddenly opened her eyes..." It was said that afterwards in the next room Rasputin collapsed into a prolonged faint due to the effort of will he had exerted. Vyrubova rapidly began her path to recovery.

Tsesarevich Alexis on the deck of a yacht. 1907.
Photograph by K.Ye. von Gan

Alexandra Fiodorovna and her son Alexis. St Petersburg. 1907

Tsesarevich Alexis with a donkey. Tsarskoye Selo. 1909. Photograph by K.Ye. von Gan

Tsesarevich Alexis on a landing-stage. Finland. 1912

Rasputin, due to her boundless faith in him, was probably the only person close to Nicholas's family who was in reality capable of restraining and calming the Empress who had lived for years on the edge of a nervous breakdown. Alexandra Fiodorovna herself confessed on several occasions that the talks with "our Friend", as she called him, gave her strength and spiritual repose. "I always remember what our Friend says. How often we fail to give sufficient attention to his words..." she wrote. All this undoubtedly endowed the "man of God" with tremendous influence that could not be harmed either by rumours of his scandalous escapades with women and revels in restaurants, or by the representations of ministers, or even by the friendly murmuring of the entire House of Romanov that developed a hatred of Rasputin.

Admittedly the tenacious idea of the omnipotence of this fateful individual whose semi-literate notes supposedly determined the entire policy of the Empire in the years immediately leading up to his death is far from the real truth of the matter. Power in the state lay in the hands of Nicholas and not Alexandra Fiodorovna and his attitude to both Rasputin and his advice was somewhat different. Although he listened to the opinions of his wife who always remained the person closest to him and although he undoubtedly valued and in his own way respected the *starets*, to whom he owed his son's life several times over, the Emperor was far from blindly executing his wishes in matters of state. Grigory did, of course, have a certain influence on him as well, but it could in no way compare with the awe in which Alexandra Fiodorovna held every word emanating from "our Friend". This difference in feelings between the Emperor and his spouse was precisely caught by the French ambassador Maurice Paléologue, who believed that Nicholas had a fairly restrained attitude towards Rasputin. Many people who were openly hostile to the *starets* remained in the Tsar's close circle, and he reacted to Rasputin's death in December 1916 incomparably more calmly than the Empress.

Yet irrespective of such subtleties, the very presence of a Siberian peasant with a widely-known scandalous reputation among the royal family gave rise to gossip and at times to malevo-

Anna Alexandrovna Vyrubova (1884–1964). 1910s

lent slander. There were, for example, rumours of a sexual relationship between Rasputin and Alexandra Fiodorovna and even her daughters that were subsequently eagerly seized upon by the printed "exposés" of the post-revolutionary years. This was a wicked slander on the royal family, but the fact that it was accepted both in the aristocratic salons of St Petersburg and among the provincial intelligentsia was an indication of how much the ancient tradition of the Russian monarchy had lost its charm and how low the prestige of the ruling dynasty had fallen in the eyes of all sections of the population. Even among the peasantry, even in the army that had always been marked by its loyalty to the throne, respect for autocratic power disappeared as it came under attack from all quarters.

NICHOLAS ROMANOV. Life and Death

These were very dangerous signs and no amount of grand celebrations intended to glorify the monarchy, and there were a great number in the last years of old Russia, could alter the situation. Magnificent festivities celebrating great jubilees in the nation's history came one after another — the 200th anniversary of the Battle of Poltava, 50 years since the liberation of the serfs in 1861, the 100th anniversary of the Battle of Borodino and, especially, the 300th anniversary of the House of Romanov in 1913. Hidden behind the facade of official events was an obscure, yet ever more evident dissatisfaction and irritation among society.

Despite the fact that in this period Russia was experiencing unprecedented economic expansion, the country's industry acquired truly European scope and level, a well-to-do peasant class was growing in the countryside, and Russian culture was flourishing in what would become known as "the Silver Age" — nothing of that was reckoned to the credit of the authorities, whereas the slightest miscalculation, failing or error in that quarter was blown up with some malevolent delight.

For all the order superficially imposed in the Empire after the smashing of the first revolution, autocratic power found itself under a sort of psychological siege. A remarkable parallel to that was the great isolation and seclusion of the life led by the imperial family who had withdrawn for good from St Petersburg society and now spent most of their time in the small, unprepossessing Alexander Palace in Tsarskoye Selo. The purely geographical remoteness of that residence symbolised, as it were, the yearning to escape from a hostile world, to find a longed-for peace in cosy family pastimes.

The Alexander Palace in Tsarskoye Selo (built in 1792–1800, architect Giacomo Quarenghi). 1910s

Nicholas II and Alexandra Fiodorovna with their children: Grand Duchess Anastasia, Tsesarevich Alexis and Grand Duchess Maria (left), Grand Duchesses Tatiana and Olga (right). 1907. Photograph by Boasson and Egger

Nicholas II's state study in art nouveau style at the Alexander Palace. Tsarskoye Selo. 1920s.

The Lilac Drawing-Room in the Alexander Palace. Tsarskoye Selo. 1920s

The imperial yacht *Standart*
on the Neva. St Petersburg.
Before 1914

Emperor Nicholas II and his
daughters on board the yacht
Alexandria. St Petersburg.
1911. Photograph by K. Bulla

Nicholas II holding
Tsesarevich Alexis on the deck
of a ship. 1906. Photograph
by K.Ye. von Gan

Saloon-car on the royal train.
1896

Nicholas II's study on the
royal train. 1896

From the memoirs of General Mosolov:
For his journeys the Tsar had two trains at his disposal.
From the outside it was impossible to tell the one from
the other: eight pale blue carriages with monograms and coats-
of-arms.
Their Majesties travelled in one of the trains, the other served, as
they say now, after the war, as camouflage. It ran empty either in
front of or behind the real royal train: even the traffic managers
had no way of knowing which of the two trains the Tsar and his
family were on.
The first carriage contained the escort and the servants.
The instant the train stopped the sentries ran to take their posts
by Their Majesties' carriages.
In the second carriage there were the kitchen and places for the
head-waiter and the chefs. The third carriage was a (mahogany)
dining-room. A third of this carriage was given over to a lounge
with heavy drapes and furniture upholstered with velvet. A piano
also stood there. The dining-room was intended to seat sixteen.
The fourth carriage was crossed through its entire width by a
corridor and was intended for Their Majesties. The first, double-
size, compartment was the Emperor's study: a desk, two

armchairs, a small library. Then came the bathroom and Their
Majesties bedroom...
The fifth carriage contained the nursery: the drapes were of fresh
cretonne, and the furniture white. The maids-of-honour were
accommodated in this carriage too.
The sixth carriage was given over to the retinue. It was divided
into nine compartments, of which one, double-size, in the middle
of the carriage was intended for the Minister of the Court.
Our compartments were far more spacious than in international
sleeping-cars. Comfort was provided, of course, at the highest
level. On each door there was a little frame to hold a visiting
card. One compartment was always left unoccupied: it was used
to accommodate people who were presented to Their Majesties
en route and for some reason remained with the train.
Finally the seventh carriage was intended for luggage, while in
the eighth there were the Inspector of the Royal Trains, the head
guard, the retinue's servants, the doctor and the pharmacy.
The court office and field office installed themselves as best they
could in the luggage van.

The ballerina Anna Pavlova. 1900s

The theatre, both in front of and behind the scenes, comprised a completely special element in the life of the imperial family: it was an enthusiasm and a passion, a regular pastime and a tribute to tradition. In his youth, overcoming a certain psychological barrier and shyness, Nicholas himself with some pleasure took the stage in a private piece of amateur theatricals, acting out scenes from *Eugene Onegin* together with Elizabeth Fiodorovna. Later, when he became Emperor, he attended dozens of performances, usually in the winter months, giving preference, like the majority of his relatives, to music and the ballet. Nicholas's favourite composer remained Tchaikovsky throughout his life and he went to his operas and ballets repeatedly.

A favourite pastime in the family of Nicholas II throughout the years was reading, quite often aloud. The Emperor himself, according to the testimony of General Danilov was brought up to twenty books a months from the library to read. Anna Vyrubova also recollected that "the Empress had an immense library of religious and philosophical works. It contained several hundred volumes and was constantly being expanded. The Empress always knew about new books from newspapers and periodicals. The task of enlarging the library was given to the court librarian Shcheglov... Sometimes during such evening reading sessions the Emperor appeared, but then he chose the book to be read... Sometimes the Emperor read aloud to us... He read superbly."
As a well-read, educated man Nicholas was by many reports an interesting conversation partner. Georgy Shavelsky, the Proto-Presbyter of the Russian Army, who frequently talked with him at Stavka during the First World War observed that "seated at table the Emperor talked without ceremony to his closest neighbours. They shared reminiscences and observations; less often scholarly questions were touched on. When they were about history, archaeology and literature, the Emperor revealed some very strong knowledge in those areas. One could not have called him unversed in the religious sphere either. He was fairly strong on the history of the Church, and also with regard to various ecclesiastical establishments and rites... The Emperor easily picked his way about serious theological questions and in generally had a correct picture of the contemporary Church... His free and easy manner and simplicity could charm absolutely anyone. One could talk with him about anything at all, talk simply, not choosing one's words, not reckoning with etiquette."

**Nicholas II's library in the Winter Palace. 1900s.
Photograph by K. Bulla**

The ballerina Mathilda Kschessinska in her mansion. 1916

Nicholas II in the uniform of the Life-Guards Cavalry Regiment with his son Alexis. St Petersburg. 1913

gymnastic exercises were ruled out. The bicycle for which Alexis repeatedly asked his parents was to remain an unattainable dream. Like many sick children he was greatly attached to pets. Frequent bouts of indisposition forced Alexis to spend the greater part of the time in bed, which gave the boy a sense of a monotonous existence. Any variety in life became an event for him. Meanwhile by his nature the heir was a fairly unruly boy. General Mosolov, who saw him quite often, would write: "I remember well how at the age of three or four he came up to the table when dessert was being served and, after hanging about by his parents, ran up to the guests and chatted easily with them with no sign of shyness. The Tsesarevich often climbed under the table, from time to time grabbing those sitting there by the leg and was delighted when it made them jump. Once he even took a shoe from one of the ladies-in-waiting and appeared with it close to his father. The Emperor scolded him and ordered him to give the shoe back immediately, which the Tsesarevich did, but again from beneath the table... Suddenly the lady-in-waiting shrieked... It turned out that the child had put a strawberry in her shoe. Of course, the feeling of something cold and wet against her foot gave her a fright. The heir was sent to his rooms and for a long time when there were guests he was not allowed into the dining-room, something he complained about bitterly. He did not crawl under the table again."

Alexis's taste for mischief was still there at a later age as is shown by the memoirs of Father Georgy Shavelsky, the Proto-Presbyter of the Russian Army, who saw him in 1915 and 1916 at Stavka: "There was a dinner with a large number of guests — it was some festival or other. I sat next to Grand Duke Sergei Mikhailovich. The Tsesarevich ran into the dining-room several times and ran out again. But then he ran in once again, with his hands behind him, and stood behind Sergei Mikhailovich's chair. The latter continued to eat, not suspecting the danger threatening him. Suddenly the Tsesarevich lifted his hands; he turned out to be holding half a watermelon without the flesh and quickly plopped that vessel on the Grand Duke's head. The liquid left in the watermelon ran down his face and its sides stuck so tightly to his head that the Grand Duke had trouble ridding himself of his unwanted hat. Try as they might, many of those present could not help laughing. The Emperor could barely contain himself. The guilty party rapidly disappeared from the dining-room..."

Incidentally, Shavelsky went on to write that "the Lord endowed the unfortunate boy with some splendid natural qualities: a powerful, quick mind, resourcefulness, a kind, sympathetic heart, the simplicity charming in princes. His spiritual beauty was matched by physical beauty."

The war brought some excitement to Alexis's rather boring life: his father often took him with him on his journeys to the front. In 1916 for visiting positions close to the front-line he was awarded the St George Medal fourth class. At the same time he was given his first military rank — corporal.

In 1917 Emperor Nicholas II took the final decision to abdicate on behalf of himself and his son only after he had received a doctor's categorical assurance that Alexis's disease was incurable.

He decided to stay with his son and devote himself to caring for him. And the sick Alexis made his last short journey — to the cellar of the Ipatyev house — in his father's arms, as Nicholas carried his heir down the stairs...

Pierre Gilliard, the Swiss tutor to Tsesarevich Alexis, and also to his sisters, recalled his pupil later: "The serious illness greatly weakened him and left him highly strung. At that time he was a child who reacted badly to any attempt to restrain him; he had never been subjected to any sort of discipline... He was quite big for his age, had a fine elongated oval face with delicate features, wonderful light chestnut hair with bronze tints, and big blue-grey eyes that reminded you of his mother's. He thoroughly enjoyed life when he could, as a lively, cheerful boy. His tastes were very modest. He did not in any way boast that he was the heir to the throne, he thought of that less than anything. His greatest happiness was to play with the two sons of the sailor Derevenko who were both somewhat younger than him.

"He had a very lively mind and judgement and could be very thoughtful. He could strike you now and then with questions too mature for his age, which were evidence of a delicate and sensitive soul. I could easily understand how those who did not have to instill discipline in him, as I did, might with no further thought succumb to his charm. Inside the capricious little creature he seemed at first, I discovered a child with a heart that was loving by nature and sensitive to suffering, since he himself had already suffered much."

The illness deprived Alexis of many joys of childhood. He could not take part in lively games with his fellows; horse-riding and

From Anna Vyrubova's book *Unpublished Memoirs:*

The grand duchesses had few friends. They entered the world of adults early, becoming accustomed to think and conduct themselves like those around them.

Grand Duchess Olga, the eldest, was more like her mother in character than the others. She was invariably just and honest... Like her mother, she was stubborn and told you to your face what she thought, at times quite sharply. As she grew up, though, that was smoothed out: she seems to have become softer, more tender and sensitive, while retaining the characteristic honesty of her early years.

You could not call Olga beautiful, her facial features were not regular — she had a small turned-up nose and her mouth was a bit large, but she had inherited her mother's golden hair, good complexion, regal bearing and grace.

Olga was probably the most talented of the Tsar's daughters. She could write very passable verses; she had musical abilities; she could play the most complicated pieces of music by ear; her voice was not strong, but pure. All the teachers were astonished by her memory, that she had, of course, inherited from her father. Nothing could distract her if she was engrossed in a task, but it was enough for her to read a lesson once or twice so as to know it by heart. Like her mother, she was very religious and was also inclined to mysticism... She was my favourite.

Grand Duchess Tatiana was very kind and restrained. She was her father's favourite. All the teachers and governesses liked her more than the other children. She never caused anybody any trouble. She always knew the wishes and demands of her parents and tried to meet them, for which the children called her the governess. She was quick and nimble... She was a skilful needlewoman and had excellent taste. Her pieces of work delighted everyone. She was entrusted with choosing presents and usually her choice proved a successful one.

Grand Duchess Tatiana had dark hair, but she was pale and, in complete contrast to her mother, never blushed. Her eyes were large and grey... When Tatiana grew up she was the tallest and most slender of all the grand duchesses, beautiful and romantic. Many men were fascinated with her. Tatiana liked to be among people more than her sisters. She often complained that she had no friends and asked me to help her strike up acquaintances. That was easier said than done — the Empress never permitted her children acquaintances that she had not approved in advance. The Empress was afraid of her daughters getting close to the aristocratic families as the children in those families were often stupidly brought up with too much freedom. The Empress did not approve of friendships with many of the grand duchesses' cousins either.

Grand Duchess Maria was a tubby girl with large eyes that shone like lamps and full lips. She was kind and obedient, but, like her younger sister Anastasia, was a forward, frisky child. It was her misfortune to be too young to be in the company of her elder sisters and not little enough to play with the two youngest members of the family. In early childhood she was very noisy and clumsy, but by the age of fourteen had become noticeably prettier... Maria loved her father more than anyone in the world and as a child was always jealous when I went for a walk with him.

Grand Duchess Anastasia was also a forward, happy-go-lucky child, clever and not without cunning — she always managed to turn things the way she wanted. With her aristocratic appearance she was closer to her mother's kin. She had long, light-coloured hair. From earliest childhood plans for different pieces of mischief sprang into her head; later she was joined by the Tsesarevich who was always ready for mischief...

Those children are still clear in front of my eyes today and much connected with them that had seemed forgotten returns again from oblivion. More vividly than anything, though, is the

The Grand Duchesses: (left to right) Maria, Tatiana, Anastasia and Olga. St Petersburg. 1914

memory of the harmony of the Tsar's family life, the tight bonds that united the members of that family.

All the children, like the parents, were of a religious and mystical frame of mind, but their chief characteristic was an ardent patriotism. Russia was so dear to them that the girls would not even contemplate a marriage outside their homeland and outside of Orthodoxy. They all wanted to serve Russia, to marry Russians and to have children who would also serve Russia.

Alexandra Fiodorovna and her retinue going to the laying of the foundation stone of the School of Folk Art on the Catherine Canal.
St Petersburg. 27 May 1914

Nicholas II with members of the family after the consecration of Kronstadt Naval Cathedral
(built 1902–13, to the design of the civil engineer Vasily Kosiakov). Kronstadt. 1913

Emperor Nicholas II and Tsesarevich Alexis with retinue inspecting detachments of the Life-Guards Chasseurs Regiment.
New Peterhof. 17 August 1912

**Emperor Nicholas II, Empress Alexandra Fiodorovna and Tsesarevich Alexis (being carried)
during celebrations of the 300th anniversary of the Romanov dynasty. Moscow. 1913**

The year 1913 began for Russia with tremendous festivities to mark a notable jubilee — the 300th anniversary of the House of Romanov. On 21 February 1613 the founder of the dynasty, Mikhail Fiodorovich, was called to rule in a ruined, depopulated land that had just emerged from the torments of the Time of Troubles. Three hundred years later, the Russian Empire, at the height of its powers and experiencing an unprecedented economic boom, celebrated the anniversary of that event with great pomp, although it was, as we now know, on the brink of another, even more terrible Time of Troubles.

Probably not one of the participants in the imperial family's journey to the historical home region of the Romanovs (the Kostroma and Suzdal area) in May 1913 could have imagined, looking at the tens of thousands of delighted people who came out onto the streets to hail their sovereign, that the dynasty would survive less than four years; that its history, which began within the walls of the ancient Ipatyev Monastery would be cut off in the cellar of the Ipatyev house in Yekaterinburg. And even a nightmare hallucination could not have suggested that the pedestal of the monument to the Romanov tercentenary, ceremonially laid at that time on the steep bank of the Volga, would be used as the base for a monument to the traitor Ulyanov, known as Lenin, who would soon put an end to the monarchy, and to the Romanovs themselves, and to the whole of Russia as it had been.

Emperor Nicholas II and members of his family on the gangplank. Yaroslavl. 1913

Nicholas II being greeted with bread and salt on his arrival as part of the celebrations
of the 300th anniversary of the Romanov dynasty. Yaroslavl. 1913

The commander of the British squadron Admiral David Beatty (second from right) with his staff. Kronstadt. 10 June 1914

Raymond Poincaré (1860—1934), President of the French Republic 1913—20, on the deck of the flagship *France*.
Petrograd. July 1914. Photograph by K. Bulla

The battleship *France* with President Raymond Poincaré aboard bound for Kronstadt
escorted by the messenger ship *Luna* and vessels of the St Petersburg port. July 1914

The fast-changing times did not give the Emperor any peace and with every year his state duties became a greater burden to him in the new conditions of political life in Russia. He was irritated by the constant interference of the Third and Fourth Dumas in the day-to-day matters of administration, the harsh, and at times unjustified criticism of the existing powers from the platform of the Duma, the endless scandals and troubles with the grand dukes of the House of Romanov who did not recognise his authority as the head of the dynasty, the hidden, yet distinctly tangible animosity of the press and the intelligentsia, particularly on the non-Russian fringes of the Empire. The familiar orderly world of his childhood, in which his father's throne had towered above the country as its unshakeable summit, was lost beyond recall. For Nicholas all that was left was love and loyalty to his own small family.

International affairs became particularly alarming in this period, threatening the ever-so-fragile calm of the Empire. Revolutions in old monarchies of Asia that had seemed set in their ways for ever — Iran, Turkey and China; the Bosnian and Moroccan crises that nearly plunged Europe into a general war; the Italo-Turkish conflict of 1911 —

all of them created a sense of an unstable existence, uncertainty in the future of Russia and of the dynasty.

In 1912 and 1913 public opinion was seriously shaken by the Balkan Wars that touched directly on Russian foreign policy tradition.

The Emperor regarded all this whirlwind of events with the same sense of doomed fatalism that had long become the psychological background to his existence. He did not try to challenge destiny, made no attempt to change the course things were taking. Only occasionally in his diary or in wholly private letters do we find suggestions that the Duma ought to be dissolved, that it ought to be turned into a purely consultative body, stripped of its legislative rights — but that all remained on paper, or the matter of rare conversations not intended for outsiders. Evidently Nicholas understood that time cannot be turned back.

And time was flowing ever faster. The shots fired at Sarajevo in the summer of 1914 heralded the final turning of the page for the old monarchic Europe. From the moment Franz Ferdinand bled to death, it plunged ever more rapidly towards its fatal finale — the First World War.

Many years later Sandro, Alexander Mikhailovich, called the day that the Great War broke out the day that European civilisation committed suicide. It did indeed mean the end not only of a system of international relations that had been decades in the making, but above all the beginning of the tremendous collapse of all the pillars of the world, the social and political foundations of the "old order", of a society that still lives by the precepts and traditions of the nineteenth century.

Emperor Nicholas had no desire for war. Apart from his innate abhorrence of military force, he knew that war could bring in its wake catastrophe for the world as he knew it. On the eve of the terrible events, in the spring of 1914, one of the most far-sighted Russian conservatives, the former Minister of Internal Affairs Piotr Durnovo, presented a memorandum to the Emperor in which he supported his main conclusion — that the approaching war between Russia and Germany would not bring victory to either side, but would destroy the monarchic principle of old Europe.

Stopping the gigantic mechanism of a European war which was picking up speed with every hour proved beyond Nicholas's power, however. Although he was prepared to make far-reaching concessions for the sake of peace, the Austro-Hungarian ultimatum to Serbia left him with no alternative. As back in 1876, the supreme power in Russia became hostage the public concern over fellow Orthodox Christians being oppressed in the Balkans. On 17 July 1914, after agonising vacillations, the Emperor confirmed the decision to begin a general mobilisation. That same day he telegraphed to the Kaiser in Berlin: "We are far from desiring war. While negotiations with Austria over the Serbian question continue, my forces will not undertake any military action. I give you my solemn word on that." Germany's response was an official ultimatum demanding that the mobilisation be halted within twelve hours. At 7.10 on 19 July 1914, the German ambassador in Russia, Count Pourtalès, a convinced opponent of war, came to Sergei Sazonov, the Minister of Foreign Affairs, with a reply. Having re-

ceived only a repeat of the former assurance that Russian troops would not begin military action first, the ambassador twice reiterated his question, after which, performing a duty that was tragic to him, he handed over the declaration of war. He was in such a state that he mistakenly gave the minister two versions of the German response — one for if Russia conceded to the ultimatum, the other if it did not. Leaving the office Count Pourtalès was crying according to Sazonov and exclaimed: "Who could have envisaged that I would have to leave St Petersburg in such circumstances!"

Nicholas, on the contrary, having taken a decision he found incredibly difficult, felt relief. "I felt that everything was over for ever between Wilhelm and me," he later told Paléologue. "I slept exceptionally soundly. When I woke up at my usual hour, it was as if a stone had slipped from my heart. My responsibility before God and the nation was enormous, but I at least knew what I had to do."

The Emperor travelled from Peterhof into the capital and after a solemn church service held in the Nicholas Hall of the Winter Palace he addressed representatives of the army and navy. When, immediately after that, he and Alexandra Fiodorovna showed themselves on the balcony of the Winter Palace, the many-thousand-strong crowd that had gathered on Palace Square felt to its knees as one.

As an extraordinary measure the State Council and the Duma which were in recess until the autumn were convened on 26 July and both legislative chambers quickly approved the laws required by the start of hostilities. There were also expressions of support from the non-Russian fringes of the Empire: even representatives of the provinces making up the Kingdom of Poland, traditionally unfriendly to Russia, formally declared their loyalty to the country and to the throne in the coming struggle with Germany. A similar declaration was made on behalf of Nicholas's subjects of German extraction. The upsurge of patriotism seen everywhere put an end to almost all partisan conflicts: yesterday's opponents of the government easily shifted to defensive positions, with

The crowd that gathered on Palace Square in anticipation of the proclamation of Russia's entry into the First World War.
St Petersburg. 20 July 1914

the exception of the Bolshevik wing of the Russian Social Democratic Party. The fact that Germany had been first to declare war on Russia encouraged the escalation of an anti-German mood that was in any case strong. As early as 22 July a jingoistic crowd wrecked and set fire to the German embassy on St Isaac's Square. In cities across the country there were mass demonstrations under the slogan "To Berlin!" At this same time the capital of the Empire turned from the Teutonic-sounding St Petersburg into Petrograd. Life in the country swiftly shifted onto a war footing.

Nicholas believed that at the hour of great trials he should personally lead the Russian army, but almost all the senior officials of the Empire came out against the idea: in the time since Peter the Great the autocrats had not usually been military commanders and the rare exceptions to the rule were associated with glaring failures. The man appointed commander-in-chief was Nicholas's first cousin once removed, Grand Duke Nicholas Nikolayevich who was popular in military circles and in the eyes of many possessed the appropriate abilities.

The building of the German Embassy on St Isaac's Square (built 1911–12, to the design of the German architect Peter Behrens). St Petersburg. 1913

Alexandra Feodorovna and Tsesarevich Alexis making the round of troops before the parade of reserve guards battalions on the Field of Mars. Petrograd. 19 April 1916

Reality rapidly wiped away the optimistic expectations of the war's first days when many looked forward to one victory after another. The advance by two Russian armies into East Prussia begun in August 1914 ended in encirclement and a resounding defeat. The commander, General Samsonov, shot himself. Russia was badly prepared for war in a military and economic sense. Industry could not provide the front with arms and ammunition in the quantities required for a world war. The situation became especially difficult in 1915 when Germany, transferring the main direction of its efforts to the East, struck a powerful blow against the Russian forces which were forced to withdraw everywhere. Under such circumstances the brief patriotic euphoria gave way to despondent disillusionment and a new outbreak of opposition.

Against a background of one failure after another at the front and growing dissent in the rear, the rumours circulating became particularly dangerous: that Rasputin held the reins of power, that the Empress was pro-German, that dubious people were up to all sorts of machinations, making their way into the court by shady routes and carrying out their treacherous intentions. Although as soon as war began Alexandra Fiodorovna and her elder daughters voluntarily began working as nurses caring for the wounded in the military hospitals of Tsarskoye Selo and performed those difficult duties with total self-sacrifice, although all talk of her treachery was deliberate lies, the public attitude towards the imperial family became openly hostile. The conviction that Rasputin, who did indeed oppose the war between Russia and Germany, was, to use the poet Alexander Blok's expression, "a convenient pedal for German spying" became very widespread in different circles.

The Time of Difficult Decisions

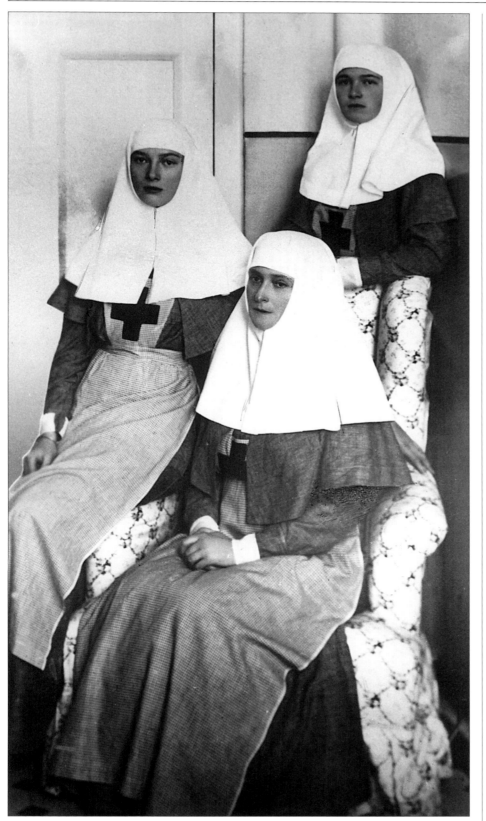

Wartime nurses — Empress Alexandra Fiodorovna with Grand Duchesses Tatiana (left) and Olga. Tsarskoye Selo. 1914. Photograph by K.Ye. von Gan

From Anna Vyrubova's book
Unpublished Memoirs:
The Empress, her two eldest daughters and I worked as nurses under the supervision of the female doctor Gedroits. Each afternoon we studied theory; each morning we worked in the hospitals.

It might be thought that our work was a kind of game, but that is far from the truth. As an example I shall take one morning when I helped the Empress and the grand duchesses, Olga, who was then nineteen, and Tatiana, who was seventeen. It needs to be said that at that moment we had only about two weeks of training behind us. We arrived at the hospital for nine in the morning and immediately went to the operating theatre to which they brought the wounded unloaded from the trains that arrived from the front. The state of those wounded men is beyond any description. They were dressed not in clothes, but in bloody rags. They were covered in dirt from head to foot; many could not tell themselves whether they were alive; they were screaming from the terrible pain. We washed our hands in disinfectant solution and set to work. First of all it was necessary to undress the wounded, or rather to take the rags and dirt off them. After that we had to wash their mutilated bodies, bathe their wounded faces, clenes the eye sockets that were often full of bloody mush. Yes, we were able to appreciate at first hand the latest methods of civilised warfare! Experienced nurses helped us with instructions and very quickly the Tsarina became a first-class nurse. I saw the Empress of All the Russias standing by an operating table with a syringe full of ether, passing instruments to the surgeon, assisting at the most terrible operations, taking amputated legs and arms from the surgeon's hands, stripping lousy clothing off the soldiers, breathing in all the stench and viewing all the horror of a military hospital in wartime, in comparison with which an ordinary hospital seems a peaceful, quiet refuge.

Since then I have seen much sorrow. I spent three years in a Bolshevik prison, but it was all nothing in comparison with the horrors of a military hospital.

The Empress told me once that the only time in her life that she felt a true feeling of pride was when she was awarded her nursing diploma. Grand Duchesses Olga and Tatiana, and I, also successfully passed the exams.

Nicholas II and Tsesarevich Alexis inspecting a unit of His Imperial Majesty's Escort bound for the front. Mogilev. 1916

From the memoirs of Pierre Gilliard *Nicholas II and his Family:*

We arrived on 16 October in Mogilev, a little Belorussian town with a very provincial appearance, to which Grand Duke Nikolai Nikolayevich had transferred Stavka two months before, during the major German offensive. The Emperor lived in the governor's house, which was built on a hill towering over the left bank of the Dnieper. He occupied two fairly large rooms on the ground floor, of which one served him as a study and the other as a bedroom. He decided that his son would live with him.

Alexis Nikolayevich's camp-bed was placed alongside his father's bed... Life settled down to the following pattern. The Emperor went off to the headquarters every day at nine and usually stayed there until 1 p.m. I used his absence to have some lessons with Alexis Nikolayevich in his study, where we were obliged to install ourselves due to the lack of premises. Lunch was served in the great hall of the governor's house. Up to thirty invited guests gathered for it each day... After lunch the Emperor dealt with urgent business, following which, about three o'clock, we went out for a drive in the car. Having come a certain distance out of town, we stopped, got out and strolled on foot through the countryside for about an hour... On his return from the trip the Emperor again got down to work, while Alexis Nikolayevich prepared his lessons for the next day in his father's study.

Nicholas II and Grand Duke Nicholas Nikolayevich (junior) on manoeuvres. Krasnoye Selo. 1913

In assuming the office of commander-in-chief on 23 August 1915, during a period of Russian defeats, Nicholas made a dangerous mistake. For his part it was the product of a profound conviction that he, the head of the Russian state, should take the tribulations of the war on his own shoulders, carrying the fighting forces with him. However, having made himself head of an army pulling back under enemy pressure, the Emperor also made himself responsible for the subsequent outcome of military operations. An even more undesirable consequence of that decision was Nicholas's move from Tsarskoye Selo to Stavka, the supreme headquarters, situated at Mogilev since 8 August. Absorbed in military concerns and the business of the front, Nicholas increasingly lost sight of how the political situation was developing in the country. Effectively his main source of information about the prevailing mood in the capital was the regular letters from Alexandra Fiodorovna in which she complained about the underhand plotting of deputies in the Duma and passed on blessings and advice from "our Friend". The Empress's highly individual perception of the world prevented her, however, from seeing the true danger.

A group of refugees with children waiting by a bakery for bread to be distributed.
Vilitko Station, Vilna province. 1914–17. Photograph by K. Bulla

Prisoners-of-war about to be sent to Petrozavodsk on board the steamer *Emperor Nicholas II*.
Petrograd. 1914–17. Photograph by K. Bulla

Soldiers of the Dukhovishchensky Regiment undergoing training in gas-masks.
The army in the field. 1915−17. Photograph by G.Z. Frid

Soldiers of the Dukhovishchensky Regiment building a field chapel.
The army in the field. 1915−17. Photograph by G.Z. Frid

Vladimir Purishkevich (1870–1920), member of the Second, Third and Fourth Dumas. Petrograd. 1916

Prince Felix Yusupov (1887–1967). Petrograd. 1914–16

In 1916, following a series of failures and short-lived ministerial appointments attributed to Rasputin's influence, the crisis of confidence in the country became obvious. After repeated attempts to make the Emperor see that such an obviously irregular state of affairs could not be allowed to continue proved futile, although they were made by Rodzianko, the chairman of the Duma, Elizabeth Fiodorovna, the Empress's elder sister, and even Nicholas's own mother Maria Fiodorovna, opponents of the "man of God" formed a conspiracy against his life. The first who tried to physically eliminate Rasputin, as early as 1915, turned out to be Alexei Khvostov, the Minister of Internal Affairs, whom ironically Rasputin had recommended for the post. He failed to carry the idea through, but in the autumn of 1916 a new group of people devoted themselves to the destruction of "our Friend".

Rasputin evoked particular hatred not so much among the opposition-minded liberals, still less among the parties of the left who saw him as a convenient target figure through whom to discredit autocratic rule, but among the last defenders of that rule — the extreme right-wing monarchists. One of their leaders in the State Duma was Vladimir Purishkevich, who in a speech to that body in November 1916 pointed out the intolerable nature of the situation that had arisen: "Rasputin is at present more dangerous than ever the False Dmitry [a pretender to the throne at the turn of the seventeenth century] was... Gentlemen ministers! If you are truly patriots, go there, to the royal Stavka, throw yourselves at the feet of the Tsar and plead for him to rid Russia of Rasputin and Rasputin's men, the great and the small."

Purishkevich's speech became the starting point for a new attempt to plan the murder of Rasputin. On the night of 16 December Purishkevich, Prince Felix Yusupov, Grand Duke Dmitry Pavlovich and a small group of others managed to achieve their intention.

On 21 November Yusupov came to Purishkevich and in effect revealed his idea of doing away with Rasputin to him.

The charming, self-assured young man quickly found an ally in the popular Duma deputy. In the course of the next few days the conspirators carefully drew up a plan of action. In order to carry it out they also enlisted Grand Duke Dmitry Pavlovich, Lieutenant Sukhotin, an officer of the Preobrazhensky Regiment, and Doctor Lazobert. Vasily Maklakov, who had made some incendiary pronouncements, refused to take part in the business, but promised, admittedly, that in the event of failure he would defend them in court. Yusupov's wife, Irina, who also knew of the plot, but was not in the city at the time, was allotted the role of "bait" — Rasputin could not resist the chance to meet the beautiful Princess. From the outset, however, events did not go the way the conspirators had planned. Neither the pies laced with cyanide, nor the poisoned Madera to which Yusupov futilely treated Rasputin had any effect, evoking an almost mystical horror in the conspirators. It was already impossible to let the *starets* go and the confederates decided to use something else. Taking a revolver, Yusupov invited Rasputin into the next room to examine a sculpture of the Crucifixion and, seizing the moment, fired almost point-blank into his side. With a cry Rasputin collapsed to the floor. The agitated conspirators, who were on the brink of hysteria, could detect no signs of life in him. Having dragged the body off the carpet onto the stone floor, they went upstairs.

As was planned, the Grand Duke, Lazobert and Sukhotin staged the departure of the "man of God". What happened next was eloquently described by those involved.

From the memoirs of Felix Yusupov:

Some time later I felt just as if something hit me. I went downstairs to where Rasputin was. He was lying in the same place, but his body was still warm. I was already on the point of leaving, but the trembling of one of Rasputin's eyelids attracted me.

I bent down. Suddenly Rasputin's eyes opened. I was frozen with terror. With a sharp movement he leapt to his feet. Foam was coming out of his mouth; a roar filled the room. His fingers dug into my schoulder, reached for my throat.

"You scoundrel!" he croaked. "Tomorrow you'll hang..."

I wanted to tear myself away from him, but I couldn't. We began to fight. Finally I managed to tear loose from his clasping hands, and he fell on the floor again, holding my torn shoulder strap in his hand. I dashed headlong out of the room calling Purishkevich. "Quickly, the revolver quickly! Shoot, he's still alive."

From the memoirs of Vladimir Purishkevich:

Yusupov appeared rushing full tilt up the stairs shouting; he literally did not have a face; his splendid big blue eyes had grown larger still and were bulging out; he was only half-conscious, almost didn't see me; with a panicstriken look in his eyes he flung himself towards the door out into the main corridor and ran through into his parent's apartment... There wasn't a moment to lose and keeping my head I pulled my *Savage* out of my pocket, took off the safety catch and ran down the stairs.

What I saw downstairs might have turned out to be a dream, if it hadn't been dreadful reality for us: Grigory Rasputin, whom half an hour before I had seen breathing his last, lying on the stone floor of the dining-room, tossing from side to side, was running quickly across the powdery snow in the palace courtyard along the iron railing that gave onto the street in the same clothes in which I had seen him almost lifeless just before. For the first instant I couldn't believe my eyes, but the loud shout he gave in the silence of the night "Felix, Felix, I'll tell the Tsarina everything" ... convinced me that it was him, that it was Grigory Rasputin, that his phenomenal vitality might let him get away... I went chasing after him and fired. In the still night the extraordinarily loud noise of my revolver carried throught the air — missed! Rasputin increased his place; I shot a second time on the run — and ... again I missed. I can't express the feeling of fury with myself I experienced at that

Grigory Rasputin. 1900s. Photograph by K. Bulla

minute. A better than decent marksman, who constantly practised on the range at the Semionovsky parade ground and hit little targets, I found myself today incapable of bringing a man down at twenty paces.

The seconds ticked by... Rasputin was already running up to the gates, then I stopped, bit my left hand with all my might to force myself to concentrate and the shot (my third) hit him in the back. He stopped, then I took more careful aim, remaining in the same place, fired a fourth time and hit him, it seems, in the head, since he dropped like a stone face downwards in the snow with his head twitching. I ran up to him and kicked him full force in the temple. He lay with his arms stretched out in front of him, scraping in the snow as if he wanted to crawl forward on his belly, but he was already incapable of moving and only chattered and ground his teeth. I was sure that now his goose was cooked and that he wouldn't rise again. After standing over him for about two minutes and convincing myself that there was no need to guard him any longer, I made my way back at the double... Yusupov's soldiers carried the body into the lobby, there by the stairs, down below. Yusupov seeing what they were about, slipped away from me... picked up a rubber dumb-bell from the desk and rushed to Rasputin's body. Having poisoned him and seen that the poison was ineffective, having shot him and seen that the bullet did not finish him, he evidently felt unable to believe that Rasputin was by now a corpse... And to my deepest astonishment Rasputin, even at that point, seems to have shown signs of life. When he was turned face upwards he wheezed and it was perfectly evident to me from above that the pupil of his right, open eye rolled, as if looking at me, senseless but awful.

Grand Duke Dmitry Pavlovich (1891–1942) in a car. 1912–14

Rumours of Rasputin's murder spread that same date. By the evening Maurice Paléologue recorded in his diary an account that had reached him by an informer of the drama that had been played out in the Yusupov Palace, correctly naming all those involved. According to his evidence, the news was already being discussed at the Yacht Club as well, inspiring, admittedly, great incredulity in Grand Duke Nikolai Mikhailovich who had supposedly already heard rumours of this kind about ten times and each time Rasputin rose up again with even more power. Nevertheless, with every passing hour the doubts faded away even among the sceptics.

The incident acquired real significance and genuine political interest, in the diplomat's opinion, from the involvement of Purishkevich. "Grand Duke Dmitry," he reflected, "is a refined man, twenty-five years old, an energetic and ardent patriot capable of displaying courage in a fight, but light-minded, impulsive and drawn into this story, it seems to me, in the heat of the moment. Prince Felix Yusupov, twenty-eight, is endowed with a lively mind and aesthetic inclinations, but his dilettante nature is too prone to unhealthy fantasies, literary images of Vice and Death; I fear that he saw Rasputin's murder first and foremost as a scenario worthy of his favourite author, Oscar Wilde. At any rate, by his instincts, face and manners he is more suited to the role of the central figure in *Dorian Grey* than a Brutus or Lorenzaccio. Purishkevich, who is already over fifty, is on the contrary a man of ideas and action. He is a champion of Orthodoxy and autocracy. He defends with strength and talent the thesis that 'the Tsar is an autocrat sent by God'. In 1905 he was chairman of the noted reactionary league 'The Union of the Russian People' and he inspired and directed terrible Jewish pogroms. His involvement in Rasputin's murder sheds light on all the conduct of the far right in recent times."

From Anna Vyrubova's book: *Pages of my Life*:

On the morning of 17 December one of Rasputin's daughters telephoned me. She told me with some alarm that their father had not come home after driving off with Felix Yusupov late in the evening... When I arrived in the palace I told the Tsarina about it. After listening to what I had to say, she expressed her bewilderment. An hour or two later a telephone call came to the palace from the office of the Minister of the Interior Protopopov, who informed us that during the night a policeman on duty near Yusupov's home had heard a shot fired in the house and rang at the door. Purishkevich had run out to him drunk and announced that Rasputin had been killed. The same policeman had seen a military vehicle with its lights switched off leaving the house soon after the shots... The Empress and I sat together, very despondent waiting for further news. First there was a call from Prince Dmitry Pavlovich who asked permission to come for tea at 5 o'clock. Pale and sad, the Empress refused. Then Felix Yusupov rang and asked permission to come and give an explanation either to the Empress or to me; he rang me several times but the Empress would not allow me to go to the telephone and said he should be told to send his explanation in writing. In the evening the Empress was brought the famous letter from Felix Yusupov in which he swore in the name of the Yusupov princes that Rasputin had not been at his house that evening. He had indeed seen Rasputin on several occasions, but not that evening. Yesterday evening he had held a party, a house-warming celebration, they had drunk too much and on the way out Grand Duke Dmitry Pavlovich had killed a dog in the courtyard.

From the Empress's telegram to Stavka at Mogilev:
We are all sitting together — you can imagine how we feel and think — our Friend has disappeared. Yesterday A. (Anna Vyrubova) saw Him and He said that Felix had asked Him to come round at night, that a car would come for Him so He could see Irina. A car did come for Him (an army car) with two civilians and He drove off. Last night there was a huge uproar in the Yusupov house — a big gathering, Dmitry, Purishkevich and so on — all drunk. The police heard shots fired. Purishkevich ran out and shouted to the police that our Friend had been killed... Felix purports not to have gone to the house and never to have invited Him. It was obviously a trap. I still pin my hope's on God's mercy, that He has only been taken off somewhere... I can't and won't believe that they've murdered him.

The body of Rasputin, killed on the night of 16 December 1916

The police established the truth fairly quickly, although the conspirators tried to disrupt the investigation in every way, presenting false evident that they had not been involved in what took place. On the third day, 19 December, in the area of Yelagin Bridge across the Malaya Nevka, Rasputin's body was found, thanks to a galosh that had fallen on the ice and gone unnoticed in the haste. The post mortem carried out without delay under the direction of Professor D.P. Kosorotov established that he had continued to live for a time beneath the water. The imperial family was perturbed.

As the evidence of the Extraordinary Commission indicates, by the evening of that same day Nicholas II had arrived in Tsarskoye Selo. "Even before his arrival, the Tsarina, exceeding her rights, gave orders for Grand Duke Dmitry and F. Yusupov to be placed under house arrest. As for Purishkevich, he had departed for the front as early as the morning of 18 December. They did not venture to arrest him, since behind him stood not only the Duma, but all the Black Hundred-monarchist camp. On the Tsarina's orders the military police only arranged to have him shadowed. Despite pressure from the Tsarina, Nicholas II did not risk bringing the aristocratic murderers to trial. Their act had evoked universal approval. The grand dukes and duchesses even addressed a collective letter to the Tsar in which they requested that Grand Duke Dmitry not be called to account. And, although Nicholas II wrote on the letter the resolution "No-one is given the right to kill", he did not venture to take decisive measures. They restricted themselves to sending Grand Duke Dmitry to the Caucasian Front, while Yusupov was banished under escort to his estate in Kursk province. "After Rasputin's body was found on 19 December it was taken to the Chesme Almshouse situated three miles outside Petrograd on the road to Tsarskoye Selo. The autopsy on the dead man discovered several firearm wounds and one large torn wound in the left side. Neither his wife, nor his daughters, nor his high-born noble admirers were allowed to take leave of him. A rumour went round the city that Rasputin's body had already been sent to his home region, to the Siberian village of Pokrovskoye, for burial. In actual fact, to avoid possible difficulties on that journey, Rasputin was temporarily buried in the Tsarskoye Selo park on 21 December. An extremely limited group of people attended the funeral: the Tsar, Tsarina, their daughters, Vyrubova, Protopopov court officials — Colonel Loman, Maltsev and the court chaplain Vasilyev, who took the service."

In the evening of that same day Nicholas wrote in his diary:
"At 9 o'clock we drove as a whole family past the photography building and to the right to a field where we played a part in a sad picture: the coffin containing the body of the unforgettable Grigory, killed in the early hours of 17 Dec. by monsters in the house of F. Yusupov, was already lowered into the grave. Father Al[exander] Vasilyev read the last rites after which we returned home..."

For the Empress the death of the *starets* was a savage blow. The British ambassador Sir George Buchanan wrote that all her hopes were concentrated on him and had now collapsed. She began to constantly fear the fulfilment of his prophesy that if he was killed the dynasty would also die. The ambassador called Rasputin's murder "a fatal error": it made the Empress more determined, made the course of possible concessions harder for Nicholas, while the people were given a dangerous example of their thoughts being turned into actions.

For the overwhelming majority, the news of Rasputin's death was cause for wild rejoicing.

"When they learnt of the death of Rasputin the day before yesterday," Maurice Paléologues wrote on 20 December, "many people hugged each other on the streets, and went to light candles in the Kazan Cathedral.

"When it became known that Grand Duke Dmitry was among the murderers, a crowd formed around the icon of Saint Demetrius to light a candle there.

"The murder of Grigory is the only topic of conversation in the endless queues of women waiting in the wind and rain outside the doors of butchers' and grocers' for the distribution of meat, tea, sugar and so on.

"They tell each other that Rasputin was thrown into the Nevka alive and express their approval with the saying: 'For a dog, a dog's death'.

"Another popular version: 'Rasputin was still breathing when they threw him under the ice of the Nevka. That's very important because that way he'll never be a saint.' The Russian people have a belief that drowned men cannot be canonised."

Felix Yusupov and his wife Irina became almost national heroes. *The Times* in Britain carried pictures of the two of them with the eloquent caption "The Saviours of Russia". Congratulations to the Russian people that had at last rid themselves of the baleful influence of "dark forces" and a "national disgrace" came flying from all quarters.

In point of fact, however, the murder of Rasputin could no longer affect anything in the political life of the country. That was evident even to many convinced monarchists. Vasily Shulgin, for example, as soon as Purishkevich let him in on the plan, expressed doubts about its effectiveness:
"If you kill him," he said, "nothing will change... Everything will remain as it is... In killing him, you won't help anything... It's too late!"

By the beginning of 1917 dissatisfaction with those in power in Russia had become almost universal. The war that had dragged on for two and a half years demanding incalculable sacrifices from the country and bringing nothing but defeats, the progressive breakdown of the transport system creating difficulties with supplies, an incredible pace of inflation — all that caused growing weariness and exacerbation with the regime. The highest circles of society were much more strongly against the autocratic state and against the Emperor personally than the broad mass of the populace. The "influence of the court clique" was far more obvious to the St Petersburg aristocracy, the heads of the Duma and the capital's intelligentsia than to millions of private soldiers at the front or the peasants of provinces far in the rear. It was the Russian elite, its patience strained to breaking point by Rasputin's grasp on power in recent months, that became the breeding-ground for all kinds of conspiracies and secret alliances aimed at removing an Emperor who had become extremely unpopular, not to say hated. Autocracy stood charged with the worst crime for any authoritarian system: complete ineffectiveness, powerlessness and inability to act for all its obvious and universally infuriating despotism.

As 1916 closed and 1917 began, all overt and covert organisations in high places in Russia — Duma factions, aristocratic clubs, high society salons, Masonic lodges and public committees were caught up in a feverish round of meetings, negotiations and agreements between people of the most different kinds connected in one way or another with the country's politics. "The present power is incapable of overcoming the chaos, because it is itself a source of the chaos. It is incapable of bringing Russia to victory in the war and therefore is inclined towards a separate peace, a humiliating capitulation to Germany" — that was the general conclusion of all political forces and groupings in Russia by February 1917.

In the capitals of the Western members of the Entente too they were looking with growing alarm at the situation at the top of their "great Eastern ally". By that time, ruling circles in those countries already had grounds to believe that they had won the Great War — an analysis of the objective balance of forces showed that Germany could not hold out more than two more years. The future of the

The Gendarmerie Building in Tverskaya Street, burnt out during the February revolution. Petrograd. March 1917

Eastern front which had tied down a considerable part of Germany's forces was, however, an evident cause for concern. Russia's capacity to continue the war was now under serious question, and that above all, in the opinion of the allies' intelligence and diplomatic services, because of its own supreme authority. The West was therefore minded to avoid an undesirable (from its point of view) course of events by carrying out with the help of Russian friends a sort of "surgical operation": to replace those in power and the existing system of government so that a new "free Russia" might become a more reliable ally in the war, and a less demanding victor at the negotiating table after hostilities were over. The instrument for accomplishing these far-reaching plans were the numerous allied missions that by then had an exceptionally elaborate network of contacts in the Russian upper echelons.

Both Russian and foreign "friends of freedom" had nothing more in mind than a change of political regimes with the help of a coup within the ruling elite, and certainly not a revolution. Memories of 1905 were too fresh for anyone to desire a repetition of that period so terrible for "law-abiding citizens". As almost always occurs in history, however, reality very quickly upset all the calculations and within a few months the period of the first revolution could easily have seemed to some a blissful idyll.

The true mechanism by which the February Revolution came about is still obscure in many of its details. A thorough study of them must be left to today's historians and tomorrow's, the visible tip of the iceberg is, however, long familiar. On 23 February 1917 the first demonstrations began on the streets of Petrograd provoked by a wave of mass dismissals and the beginnings of disruptions to the bread supply. The military authorities in the capital were unable to take control of the situation immediately and within three days it was no longer possible: the troops refused to obey orders and fraternised with the demonstrators. The second Russian revolution had become a reality.

Emperor Nicholas, who was at Stavka, clearly missed the critical moment in the unfolding events. During those few decisive days when strikes and demonstrations were turning into a full-blown revolution, he continued to concern himself with the immediate affairs of the moment, failing to grasp the nature of what was taking place. When, on 27 February, the existing power in Petrograd effectively collapsed and the State Duma tried to take on the role of intermediary, putting forward a proposal for a "responsible government", the Emperor resolved to take harsh measures to restore order, not recognising that the time had irrevocably passed. As a result the expeditionary force that he despatched to the capital under the command of General Ivanov on 28 February could not get through because of the paralysis of the railways

gripped by strikes and the mass disintegration of units that had even recently seemed reliable. The same fate befell the two trains in which Nicholas, accompanied by his suite, had set off for Tsarskoye Selo. They were forced to turn back to Pskov, where the headquarters of the Northern Front was situated. While the Emperor was wandering around the railway system, further irreversible changes took place in the situation.

By 1 March, the majority of generals who had command of armies realised that events had moved on: Rodzianko informed them from Petrograd that "responsible government" was no longer sufficient to calm the revolutionary storm. Circles in and around the Duma came to the conclusion that only Nicholas's immediate abdication could save the monarchy in Russia. With this aim a special mission of deputies Alexander Guchkov and Vasily Shulgin set off for Pskov on the morning of 2 March. That same day telegrams arrived in Pskov from the commanders of the various fronts. Almost unanimously they supported the call for Nicholas's abdication. Apart from a few people personally close to the Tsar, like the Count Fredericks, long-time Minister of the Court, everyone demanded that he went.

Demonstration on Liteiny Prospekt. Petrograd. 1917

On the evening of that same day Nicholas handed the signed manifesto on the abdication to Guchkov and Shulgin. He renounced the throne on behalf of himself and his son Alexis. Subsequently many were surprised by the strange calm, even detachment, with which the Emperor laid down the supreme power that he had assumed almost a quarter of a century before. Some saw the reason as lying in his exceptional self-control; others in his profound indifference to the fate of

Alexander Fiodorovich Kerensky (1881–1970), the head of the Provisional Government, in the library of the Winter Palace. Petrograd. 21 August 1917. Photograph by K. Bulla
After heading the Labour group in the Fourth State Duma, in March 1917 he joined the Provisional Government as a representative of the Social Revolutionaries. Until May he had charge of the Ministry of Justice, later of the War and Navy Ministry, before assuming the post of prime minister in July. After the Kornilov mutiny he also became commander-in-chief of the Russian army. Following October 1917 he lost all support in Russia and emigrated. He died in the USA.

Yuri Miliutin (seated), Vice-Chairman of the St Petersburg City Duma, and Alexander Guchkov, member of the State Duma. 1913

Vasily Shulgin (1878–1976), deputy of the State Duma. 1910s

Packing up paintings in the rooms of the Catherine Palace at Tsarskoye Selo after the departure of Nicolas II and his family.
Tsarskoye Selo. October 1917

the nation. It would seem, however, that Nicholas's calm had a different cause: as a sincere Christian he regarded the whole matter as the ineffable will of God that should be accepted with due humility. He had performed his duty with dignity and to the last, the rest did not depend on him. The best evidence that what had taken place was not a matter of indifference to him comes in the diary entry for 2 March which ends with words full of bitterness: "Left Pskov at 1 a.m. with a heavy feeling from the experience. Treachery and cowardice and deceit all around!"

Nicholas spent another week in Mogilev, in the familiar surroundings of Stavka. Dowager Empress Maria Fiodorovna came from Kiev for a few days to see her son. We shall never know now what they talked about in those March evenings passed drinking tea or playing cards. For all the apparent humdrum nature of those days they were full of hidden tragedy — each of them was marked by meetings with close companions, relatives and assistants that were destined to be the last in his life. And his parting from his mother, as she returned to Kiev, proved to be for ever...

"We shall not assess and judge here the deeds of the former sovereign: a dispassionate judgement on him belongs to history, while he now stands before the impartial court of God, but we know that when abdicating the throne he did so with a view to Russia's benefit and out of love for her. He could have found himself security and a relatively peaceful life abroad after the abdication, but he did not do that, desiring to suffer together with Russia. He undertook nothing to better his situation, submitted uncomplaining to fate..."

From the Sermon on the Killing of the Royal Family *given by Tikhon, Patriarch of Moscow and All Russia, in the Cathedral of Our Lady of Kazan, Moscow, on 8 (21) July 1921*

Epilogue

The last photograph in this book... Prematurely aged and lonely, tired and sad, Nicholas looks out at us, as if bidding farewell to the reader. He still had almost a year and a half to life, but his role in the centre stage of history was over — from now on others, contemporaries and those who came after, would have their say.

Now, when the years of power were irrevocably a thing of the past for him, fate granted the former Emperor and his family a few last months of domestic cosiness. On 9 March Nicholas arrived by train from Stavka at the Tsarskoye Selo station, returning to his expectant wife, daughters and beloved son. He was no longer the monarch, an actor in and creator of history, but remained the head of a family tenderly devoted to him and its joys and sorrows were for him now the only meaning of existence. Until August 1917 they continued to live in the Alexander Palace at Tsarskoye Selo. Nothing changed in the life within the family, except that the father for the first time had the opportunity to devote his days entirely to it. He continued to read a lot, giving preference to historical and historical-political works: in those months, for example, he read the *History of the Byzantine Empire* by Academician Fiodor Uspensky and *The Tasks of the Russian Army* by the former Minister of War Alexei Kuropatkin, both of which had been published a few years before. Nicholas enjoyed spending time with the growing Alexis, often worked in the garden and prayed at length for Russia and for victory in the war. This quiet, gently paced existence wholly accorded with the character of the former autocrat, if it had not been for one thing: the family found themselves under house arrest. As early as 20 March the Petrograd Soviet had resolved "to deprive Nicholas Romanov and his spouse of their freedom" and a disturbing uncertainty hovered over them, a foretoken of the tragic end.

Originally it was assumed that the imperial family would leave the country and live in Britain, or possibly Denmark, whose ruling houses were linked to the Russian one by ties of close kinship. However, in the circumstances of a world war that had split Europe into two opposing camps engaged in a struggle to the death, that proved impossible: not one of the possible host countries found it desirable to receive the family of the former Emperor. The negotiations that the Provisional Government conducted on the matter ended without result. In essence, though, their fate was settled by the frame of mind dominant at that time in almost all the revolutionary camp, which was expressed well by one of the leaders of 1917, the Menshevik Nikolai Chkheidze. In response to Rodzianko's suggestion that the Tsar and his family should be sent abroad, he remarked: "Never. He has enormous sums of money there — 500 million roubles in gold. He'll organise such a counter-revolution for us that nothing will be left of us. He has to be rendered harmless here..."

Meanwhile, time was working against the deposed Romanovs. The heightening of tension in the country in the summer of 1917 and the stirring up of hatred against the former rulers which became a propaganda weapon for the revolutionary parties made the family's continued presence in the Alexander Palace risky. Their proximity to fermenting Petrograd was a danger factor to them themselves and created extra difficulties for the Provisional Government. In August 1917 Nicholas and those close to him were sent under heavy guard to Tobolsk in Siberia, a place that had not yet been seized by revolutionary passions. A day before their arrival there, they were able to see from the deck of the river steamer Rasputin's home village of Pokrovskoye. Another of the *starets's* prophesies had come true: at one point he had told Alexandra Fiodorovna that before she died she would go there.

In the Tobolsk governor's house specially refurnished for their arrival, an 18-room mansion standing in a garden with electricity and running water, the family of the last autocrat spent several peaceful months. But changes were taking place in Russia's destiny that would prove fatal to them — the implacable and merciless enemies of all that the Romanov dynasty stood for came to power in the country.

From the spring the regime under which the Tsar's family were being held grew sharply worse. Petty nuisances and insulting tricks of all sorts grew more frequent. The Bolsheviks plainly stated that the finale for "Nicholas the Bloody" and his family should be an open public trial. A few trials of this kind, where the accused had participated in the suppression of earlier revolutionary actions, were held in 1918 and invariably ended in the passing of death sentences, giving an example of popular justice in action. Fate, however, had another, albeit no less tragic, end in store for Nicholas and his loved ones. There is much in the history of their last months that is mysterious and still not cleared up by researchers. In April 1918 the family escorted by the detachment of Vasily Yakovlev, the special representative of the All-Russian Central Executive Committee were removed from Tobolsk to go to Moscow for a public trial. They were stopped at Yekaterinburg, however, by a decision of the Bolshevik leadership of the Urals Regional Soviet who pointed to the danger from the White Guards. After that the questions begin — questions that are as hard to answer with complete certainty even now.

The main one is the nature of the political game being played between Moscow and Yekaterinburg in those three months when open civil war broke out in the country. In May 1918 the Bolshevik party Central Committee discussed the further fate of the imperial family who were by then already in the Urals: "It is necessary to decide what to do with Nicholas. The decision was taken not to undertake anything with regard to Nicholas for the moment, taking care only that the necessary security measures are implemented. Sverdlov was entrusted with discussing this with the Urals people."

The leadership of the Urals Regional Committee, headed by Alexander Beloborodov, was notable for its particularly uncompromising attitude towards the deposed monarch. Nicholas himself when he learnt the route of his last journey said: "I would go anywhere at all, only not to the Urals... Judging by the newspapers, the Urals are strongly opposed to me..." It might be said that the imperial family were condemned to death by the very fact of being moved to Yekaterinburg. The only thing that is unclear is who ultimately sanctioned their execution in the cellar of the house belonging to the mining engineer Ipatyev on the night of 16 July 1918. Was the decision taken in Moscow by the Bolshevik leadership of the country under Lenin and Yakov Sverdlov, or was it the individual initiative of the Urals Bolsheviks? Despite the fact that in recent years many researches specially devoted to the

Yekaterinburg tragedy have been published, there is still no definitive answer. One can, incidentally still find people who insist that there was no killing in Yekaterinburg at all, and the most varied and at times incredible stories are told about the subsequent life of Nicholas and his family.

When the seemingly unshakeable, age-old Russian monarchy disappeared in February 1917, like some wraith or phantom, without really showing any resistance, nobody mourned over its glorious past. Nobody, apart from a very small number of people who knew and loved Nicholas and his family, sensed the Emperor's personal tragedy either. Not even the terrible end in Yekaterinburg, which became common knowledge before the summer of 1918 was out, could change the universal dislike surrounding the ruling Romanovs. Already in emigration, many of the leading influences of the past era, reflecting on the causes of the Russian catastrophe, placed the blame squarely on the last Emperor. Zinaida Gippius, a confirmed enemy of Bolshevism, wrote of him that "they left Nicholas Romanov like an empty spot." Even sincere monarchists reckoned that the Emperor had proved a failure as a man and as a ruler.

But the further the years of his life and reign disappeared into the past, the fewer witness there were of that age and the more historians, the greater the understanding and respect with which Nicholas was written and spoken of in the Russian community abroad. The tragedy of the man set aside in the eyes of the new generation the inadequacies of the autocrat.

It is a curious fact that the attitude to Nicholas in Soviet society also changed in a similar manner. The furious insults and abuse heaped upon him in the first years after the revolution gave way to a restrained silence. While at one time schoolchildren were taken on excursions to the cellar of the Ipatyev house and the murderers of the royal family proudly related their "revolutionary feat" by the campfires of pioneers, surrounded by the admiring young generation, in the 1970s this incident was mentioned with embarrassed brevity or exonerating explanations. Things went so far that the Ipatyev house itself was demolished so as there would be no historical reminder...

A dispassionate view comes with the passing of time. Contemporaries are unable to divorce themselves from the evils of the day, the impressions and psychological traumas of events still fresh. The great Roman historian Tacitus once wrote of this law of human memory: "The deeds of Tiberius and Gaius, Claudius and Nero were falsely presented while they were all-powerful, under the influence of fear and servility towards them; and when they had passed on, under the influence of the still-fresh hatred they had left towards themselves." In order to write about historical events and historical figures "without anger and bias", the brilliant creator of the *Annals* informs us, a chronicler needs a certain temporal distance — a year, ten, thirty, fifty years... for complete objectivity — a whole century. That is how they thought in the Ancient World — the time to examine the affairs of past generations without prejudice comes only when the last witness to them has departed this life...

In recent days the question of the fate of the last Emperor and his family has again become the focus of public attention. Like a select few figures in Russian history, Nicholas II has become both man and symbol, whose life and death continues to trouble the hearts and minds of millions of his fellow-countrypeople. What is he when the balance is drawn? — doomed victim or the chief culprit in the Russian catastrophe of 1917. The answer has many sides to it and each of us decides which to see depending on his or her historical sympathies and antipathies, personal convictions or the opinions predominating in society. Here we would only wish to draw the reader's attention to the words of Metropolitan Anastasius spoken in Jerusalem, at Golgotha, in the Church of the Holy Sepulchre, on the seventh anniversary of the imperial family's death:

"We know that people, like precious metals, show their true selves in the crucible of fiery testing. The late Emperor went through both the main forms of temptation to which a man is subject on Earth: the temptation of superiority, glory and happiness, and the temptation of humiliation, privations, mental and physical suffering. It is hard to say which of these courses of temptation is the more dangerous for us. It is hard for a man to bear the awareness of his superiority to other people and to stand firm against the intoxicating effect of majesty, glory and wealth that almost always come to him in the company of their inseparable companion in the form of the temptation of pride. No less moral effort is demanded of us to preserve a calm greatness of spirit when heavy sorrows and misfortunes afflict us, when the human heart unintentionally rages against the whole world or falls into despondency... The throne of the Russian Tsar at the time when it was inherited by Emperor Nicholas II stood so high that it was visible to the whole world: yet its glitter did not blind the late sovereign for a minute. He did not become drunk with the wine of power and was not fascinated with his own transient majesty. On the contrary, he was rather burdened by it and unable to overcome his innate feeling of modesty that frequently hindered him from displaying his power to the extent that the circumstances of the time now and then demanded...

"Like Job, on whose day it was the will of God that the Emperor came into the world, he was stripped in a single instant of glory and wealth, realm and friends. Only a few of those close to him wanted to drink the cup of suffering with him and remained loyal to him to the end. Others, although they sympathised with his miserable state, did not venture to declare themselves openly, so as not to be separated from the crowd... The Lord granted the long-suffering Emperor only one consolation comparable with Job — that was a loving family selflessly devoted to him, but, alas, they had to share with him nothing but humiliations and sorrows, and so sometimes became for him the involuntary source of new sufferings...

"Held under arrest the sovereign must have experienced all the bitterness of lack of freedom and all the harshness of human ingratitude. People who had only recently trembled at his single glance and seized on his smile like a life-giving ray of the sun, now subjected him to the coarsest of insults, and mocked not only him and the Empress, but also their young children fragrant with tender purity... Yet not one word of complaint about his lot issued from the lips of the royal sufferer. He resembled the One of Whom it is written: being slandered, he never slandered in return; suffering, never threatened... To God alone did they proclaim their sorrow and before Him alone did they pour out their hearts. The feeling of abandonment that oppressed their spirits did not cool their love for Russia: forgetting their own trials, the royal prisoners continued to the last to live and suffer inseparable from their people..."

CONTENTS

NICHOLAS ROMANOV
Life and Death

ISBN 5−87417−065−0
LR №070890 of 14 May 1998
Run: 7000.

Liki Rossii Publishing Firm
17/8, per. Pirogova,
190000, St Petersburg, Russia.
Tel.: (812) 312 1121. Fax: (812) 312 3897.